THE GRAND TOUR

A 90-day prayer journey across the continent of Asia

10 Publishing
a division of 10 of those.com

ASIA LINK.

First published in Great Britain in 2022

British Library Cataloguing in Publication Data
A record for this book is available from the British Library

ISBN: 978-1-914966-58-3

Designed by Pepper Collective

10Publishing, a division of 10ofthose.com
Unit C, Tomlinson Road, Leyland, PR25 2DY, England
Email: info@10ofthose.com
Website: www.10ofthose.com

Printed in Denmark
1 3 5 7 10 8 6 4 2

PREFACE

Let all the earth fear the Lord;
let all the people of the world revere him.
For he spoke, and it came to be;
he commanded, and it stood firm.
(Ps. 33:8–9)

How great is our world! How vast! How awesome! And how great is the One who made all the world, speaking it into being! At the Lord's command, creation continues to stand firm. Generation after generation has spent much time and many resources exploring the extent, variety and beauty of all that God has made, and yet there remains so much to discover. How great is the task, then, of us getting to grips with Asia, just one of this wonderful world's continents, as we 'journey' over the next 90 days. By travelling the length and breadth of the continent, our goal is to explore the vast array of people and cultures living in God's world, to understand how He is at work among them, and to lift up those who are lost in powerful and passionate prayer.

Time will be far too short to explore the beliefs and customs of every one of Asia's many people groups. We will not visit every city, or even every country, and yet this journey offers an opportunity for us all. Here before each of us lies a chance to explore, discover, learn and grow, not just in our knowledge of places and peoples, but in our understanding of the Lord's purposes for them and for us.

As we embark on this adventure, a lot will be familiar to us. The scenery will vary from tropical islands to frozen tundras, and from gleaming white snow on mountain peaks to lush green paddy fields in expansive valleys. We will experience cultures shaped and defined by major belief systems such as Buddhism, Hinduism and Islam, as well as groups which hold Shinto, communist and animist beliefs at their core. We will meet the young and the old, the rich and the poor, the saved and the lost.

Still, there will be much to surprise us along the way. Who can say which places will inspire us, whose stories will move us and what truths the Lord will teach us as we explore this part of His world? We cannot predict the ways in which He might speak to us and shape our hearts in the days ahead.

As we step out on this journey, let us do so in faith, prayerfully and thoughtfully reflecting on every sight, sound and story, and seeking the Lord at every turn.

Let all the earth fear the Lord;
let all the people of the world revere him.

DAY 1

DAY OF PREPARATION

In the final rush before any adventure begins, the panic starts to set in. Have I packed enough clothes? Did I buy the right toiletries? What time do I need to get to the airport? Checking the pocket where your passport should be, you breathe a sigh of relief that it is still there, as it was the previous five times. You print another copy of your itinerary, just in case you lose the other three. Finally, plane tickets in hand, you walk out of the door and climb into your taxi.

After the mad rush comes a moment of contemplation. Your trip has been prepared – flights, meetings, hotel bookings ... Your bag has been prepared too, bursting at the seams with t-shirts and socks, soap and sanitiser. But what about your heart? Are you truly ready for all that lies ahead? Are you ready to listen, learn, absorb and reflect? Are you ready to be taught, challenged and shaped by the places and people you will encounter? Are you ready to commit every place, person, thought and feeling into the hands of the One who will oversee your journey?

Perhaps that thought is new to you, and a little scary. Perhaps you know you should do this, but it remains an unmastered discipline. Welcome to the club! We are all so easily distracted by the good things of this world that we forget the One who made them and upholds them. So now is the time to bring your heart before the Lord. Commit it into His hands. Commit *yourself* into His hands! He is faithful in all He does, and the earth is full of His unfailing love (Ps. 33:4–5).

BIBLE VERSE

'... the earth is full of his unfailing love' (Ps. 33:5).

REFLECTION

Turn to Psalm 33 and take a few moments to reflect on what it says about the Lord, about the world He has made, and about the nations and peoples who inhabit it. As you journey, you will encounter many people whose plans and purposes will one day be thwarted by the Lord (v. 10). You will also meet those He has chosen for His inheritance – your brothers and sisters in Christ. In some cases, these will be workers who can openly and freely declare the good news to their neighbours. Elsewhere, the lives of believers will be a powerful demonstration of what it means to live in the hope of deliverance, waiting for the Lord and trusting in His holy name (vv. 18–22). Is your heart ready to be challenged as you meet those who oppose the Lord, and as you witness the struggles faced by those who call Him 'Father'?

PRAYER

Lord, I commit to You the adventure which lies ahead. Thank You for this wonderful world which You have made, and for the many nations, cultures and people found within it. I pray that as I travel around Asia over the next 90 days, You would go with me. Help me to seek You at every turn and to hear Your voice. I pray that Your Spirit would be at work in me, teaching me, helping me grow and softening my heart so that it might become more like Yours.

DAY 2

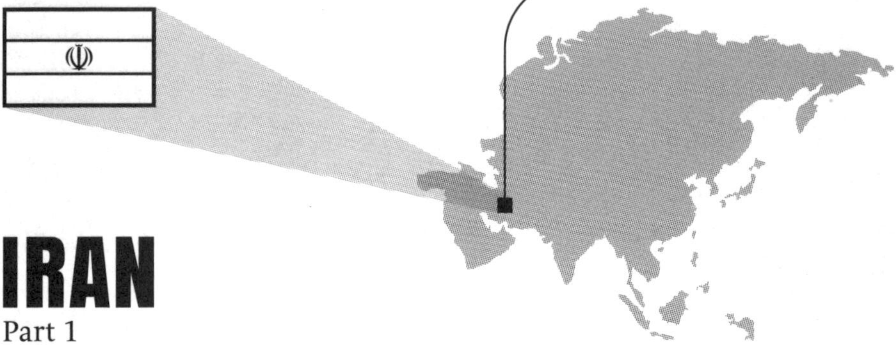

IRAN
Part 1

The plane is descending towards your first stop on this incredible journey. Looking out of the window, you are struck by the sight of the Milad Tower, which stands tall over the city. Its long needle, reaching up into the sky, passes in and out of your vision in the blink of an eye. The tower is perhaps the most famous and iconic image of the city of Tehran, Iran's capital.

In many ways, the city is just as you imagined, aligning with the impression formed in your mind from news reports back home. As you expected, it's hot. Very hot. Your bag sticks to your back as you make your way through streets thronging with bearded men, armed police officers and women in hijabs. You catch the eye of one of these women as you walk and try to imagine life in her shoes. Is she happy and content? Is she resolute in her obedience to her husband and local imam, or does she quietly long for something else?

In the distance, you spot a man apprehending another woman wearing a hijab. She's being told to wear her headscarf more respectfully – beneath it, her hair was streaming over her clothes. The man must be part of Tehran's morality police. While their numbers have decreased in recent years, many still patrol the streets, enforcing rules such as women being required to cover their heads in public. The morality police are just one example of the oppressive Islamic regime which governs this nation. However, much greater infringements to liberty are committed here. While great swathes of the Old Testament depict events within its borders, Iran now ranks among the ten worst countries in the world for persecution against Christians.

BIBLE VERSE

'He upholds the cause of the oppressed and gives food to the hungry. The Lord sets prisoners free' (Ps. 146:7).

REFLECTION

In the West, freedom is easily taken for granted. With many freedoms enshrined in law, we are largely allowed to say what we like without fear of recrimination, and to believe what we wish without fear of such persecution. Even more significantly, as believers we are free from the eternal consequences of sin. The punishment for our iniquities has been borne by the Lamb, setting us free to love, worship and serve Him. Psalm 146 reminds us that the Lord is concerned with the plight of the oppressed. Iranian believers can take comfort in the knowledge and presence of a Father who hates oppression and injustice. We long for a day, though, when all Iranians are set free not just from earthly oppression, but also from the burden of sin. As we pray for that day, how will we use our freedom for His glory?

PRAYER

Lord, thank You for the freedom I have in You. I pray that You would burden my heart so that I make the most of the freedoms I enjoy to be a part of Your work in furthering Your kingdom. Thank You for Your Son, for His sacrifice and for the forgiveness I have received. Lord, I pray for those who are oppressed in Iran. Please bring both earthly and spiritual freedom to this land, so that Your name would be glorified.

DAY 3

IRAN

Part 2

It is strange making your way around a country with such a well-publicised and turbulent past, though you would never know it as you explore the city. The streets are full of people living normal lives – shoppers bustling between various outlets, women chatting in the street and a group of boys noisily playing football against a wall. However, it wasn't all that long ago that these same streets were filled with protesters and mourners following the assassination of one of Iran's most popular generals. For a few days in 2019, the whole world held their breath as tensions rose between Iran and the US.

The revolution in 1979 transformed this land. The Shah was seen by many as an oppressor who was too friendly with America. Discontent grew amid economic struggles and perceived marginalisation of the true Islamic faith. The revolution put in place a new leadership and government. Suddenly, the moderate and modernising Shah-led nation became ground zero for a Shia Islamic revival. Thousands, in fear, fled to safety outside of the country, while Iran also quickly became one of the most difficult places on earth to follow Jesus Christ. To this day, the church meets underground, the Bible is a difficult book to obtain and the gospel cannot be shared openly.

You stop in the street outside a mosque. Men and women are filing in through two separate doors, removing their footwear and washing themselves in preparation for prayer. You can hear the low murmur of prayer to Allah from beyond the doors. Your heart hangs heavy in your chest as you wonder whether those inside will ever hear the gospel.

BIBLE VERSE

'He rules for ever by his power, his eyes watch the nations – let not the rebellious rise up against him' (Ps. 66:7).

REFLECTION

It can be tempting to believe that places like Iran will never change. Severe opposition to the Christian faith can lead us to wonder how God's kingdom could ever be proclaimed here. Psalm 66 reminds us that the Lord still rules – even in places where it doesn't look that way. The nations are carefully considered by Him. He watches them, rules over them and, by His Spirit, still works for His glory through them. If humankind was able to turn Iran upside down in the Iranian Revolution, surely our Almighty God can turn it right side up again? There is always hope to be found in our Lord.

PRAYER

Lord, thank You for Your concern for the nations in our world. You watch them and nothing that happens is beyond Your sight. I praise You for Your sovereignty; nothing is beyond Your control. Lord, I'm sorry for when I believe things will never change. In You, all things are possible. I pray that Iran would be opened up to the gospel, so that Christ might be proclaimed and churches might meet openly for Your glory!

DAY 4

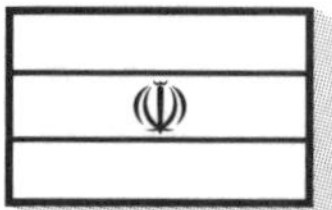

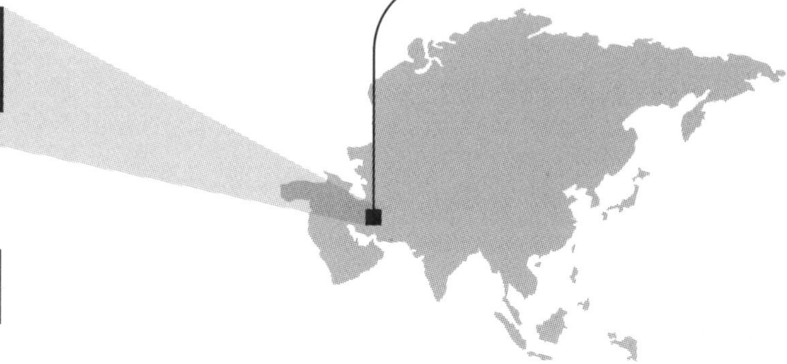

IRAN

Part 3

As you speak with young adults and students, you begin to identify a sense of hopelessness. They don't seem particularly proud of their nation. In fact, many are keen to highlight the issues plaguing their land. They speak of widespread unemployment; millions are out of work and thousands of young people are leaving the country in search of opportunities elsewhere.

New friends also tell you about Iran's pressing drug problem. Estimates of the number of addicts range from two and a half million right up to seven million. As a result, Iran has one of the highest incarceration rates in the world. Most of the prison population have been incarcerated for drug-related offences. With all these factors in play, an acute sense of emptiness and futility seems to have settled into Iran. Sadly, this is evidenced by a rise in suicides, with a 66% rise among women and a 71% increase among men. You wonder if these are signs of a God-forsaken land.

A contact leads you to a local church meeting in secret, but which has grown rapidly in recent years. As you step into the small house, it is filled wall to wall. Remarkably, despite its fierce opposition to the gospel, Iran is currently home to the fastest-growing church in the world. There are many protests in Iran against the regime, with people wanting to be not an Islamic Republic but an Iranian Republic. There is a strong and growing desire for freedoms of press, of speech and even of belief. But more significantly, the hopelessness you detected among the people of Iran has led many to recognise Islam for what it is: an empty and false religion. God is moving here, bringing thousands to Himself. Praise God there is hope for Iran!

BIBLE VERSE

'Then will the eyes of the blind be opened and the ears of the deaf unstopped'
(Is. 35:5).

REFLECTION

The deep sense of discontentment that is evident in Iran is truly remarkable. The country's influence and power make it appear untouchable, while the Islamic regime and oppressive attitude towards Christianity can make it seem impenetrable with the gospel. Not to our Lord! As ever, He is working behind the scenes, orchestrating events by His power in order to make His name known and bring glory to Himself. His actions are stirring people's hearts. Long-shut eyes are being opened to the falseness of Islam and long-closed ears are opening to the truth of His Word. Without a doubt, the Lord *is* building His church in Iran. Hallelujah!

PRAYER

Lord, I praise You as the only hope for this world. When all seems lost, when the enemy appears to be winning, You are still watching and working for Your glory. Lord, I delight with those in heaven at the growth of Your church in Iran. Thank you for opening the eyes of the blind and the ears of the deaf. I pray for Your continued blessing on the people here. Please would many more come to know Your Son as their own Lord and Saviour!

DAY 5

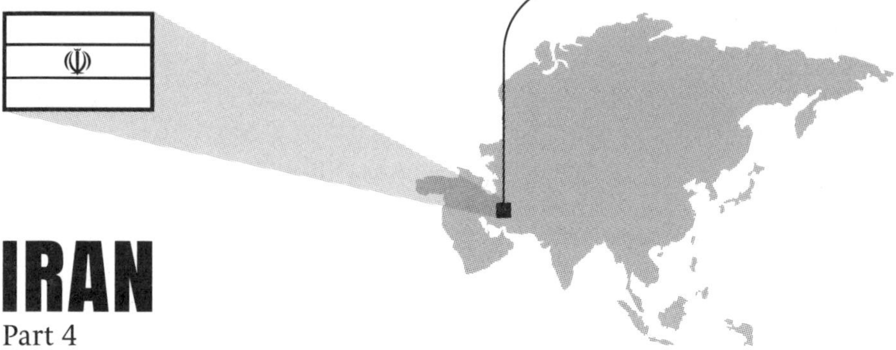

IRAN

Part 4

Over these short few days in Iran, you have learned of opposition to Jesus Christ and His followers. Yet you have also encountered a number of believers striving to faithfully serve the God they love. The church is exploding in size and believers have been filled with joy at what the Lord is doing. Older Christians remember church leaders who longed to see days like these, many of whom were martyred by the government – killed for their faith yet rejoicing in heaven!

You discover that several recent converts share a similar testimony. Each had encountered evangelists giving out gifts in the street, sometimes in Iran and at other times on holiday elsewhere. The gifts were small SD cards which, when inserted into a smartphone, provided access to incredible truths that the converts had never discovered. They heard worship songs in their own language, watched videos explaining the truths of Christianity and read a digital copy of God's Word! Confronted with the gospel, and after conversing safely with evangelists online, these young adults put their faith in Christ, then were connected to a local church.

One woman has the card on her and pulls it out. It's no bigger than a fingernail but is the greatest gift she has ever received because, through it, she learned that Christ gave His life for her. You take the little card in your hand, marvelling at the power of God to bring new life to so many from such a tiny piece of technology. Thousands of these cards have been distributed over the years and it is impossible to number those who may have accessed the gospel through them. Only in heaven will we discover how many lives have been transformed in this way!

BIBLE VERSE

'He told them another parable: "The kingdom of heaven is like a mustard seed, which a man took and planted in his field. Though it is the smallest of all seeds, yet when it grows, it is the largest of garden plants and becomes a tree, so that the birds come and perch in its branches"'
(Mt. 13:31–32).

REFLECTION

The power of God is truly marvellous to behold. How remarkable it is to consider the vast fruit that has been produced by God's grace through those SD cards. In Matthew 13, Jesus depicts the kingdom of heaven as a mustard seed. It is a seemingly insignificant seed, unimpressive in its appearance, and yet it grows to become one of the largest plants in the garden with birds perching in its branches. In the same way, with the Lord's help, these tiny SD cards have contributed so much to the extension of God's kingdom in Iran and elsewhere. May many more discover the truth of the Lord through them!

PRAYER

Lord, thank You for technology and for those You have gifted with the skills to develop it. Thank You for using technology to open doors for the gospel in places where they were previously closed. Lord, I pray that You would continue to use the creativity of believers to multiply Your church, and ready the hearts of Iranian Muslims to receive the gospel however it reaches them. Thank You that so many lives have already been saved here by Your grace. Please sustain new converts and strengthen their faith.

DAY 6

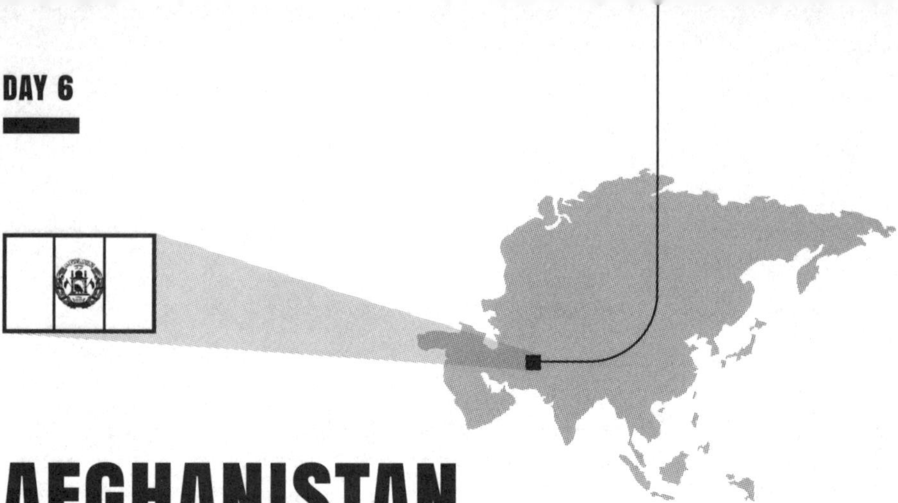

AFGHANISTAN

Part 1

Your attention turns from the steady hum of the jet engines to the blue sky stretching above the white-topped mountains. In the near distance, you trace the line of Kabul airport's runway just north of the city, surrounded by brown hills. Once again, a mixture of feelings sweeps over you: excitement but also fear due to the turmoil you know is affecting this land.

Of the world's 26 million refugees, several million are Afghans who have fled regions where conflict has been a near constant for years. After the Taliban had been ousted in 2001, responsibility for the country's security was handed to Afghan forces in 2014, before the Taliban's sudden resurgence. As a result, opportunities for education, for settled farming and for prosperity have all been lost. Many consider Afghanistan to be a lawless, ungovernable region, best left to its own devices. You wonder whether this visit will cause you to agree.

As you travel towards the city, you gaze from the bus window. Trees line the busy road as men dressed in white shalwar kameez ride decrepit bicycles between the traffic. By the roadside, rickshaw stalls sell huge yellow-green watermelons beneath fading red plastic sheets. Your thoughts are abruptly interrupted by a muezzin's song, amplified and crackling through the loudspeaker, calling the faithful to prayer. This country is full of hospitable and charming people. However, extreme forms of Islam are pervasive, with deviation from the majority faith not entertained lightly. This is perhaps one of the greatest paradoxes of this beautiful, ruggedly austere nation.

Though numbers are small, the church exists here. There were believers in each of the 34 provinces before the Taliban returned. It is hard to know exactly how many remain, given that the death penalty is a real threat for all who follow Christ.

BIBLE VERSE

'But for you who revere my name, the sun of righteousness will rise with healing in its rays' (Mal. 4:2).

REFLECTION

The land of Afghanistan has known the scars of strife for years. Its mostly young population has known nothing but a time of war and rumours of war. Yet God promises healing and peace for those who fear His name. There is healing through the Son of God, both now and on that promised final day which will dawn on every land in this world. The sun of God's righteousness will rise and cast healing light on all who turn their gaze towards Him. Jesus has not overlooked Afghanistan but instead promises to build His church among its rugged hills. He will not be denied; He will triumph over all the earth. May we be people who accelerate the return of the Lord Jesus as we hold out good news to every nation!

PRAYER

Lord, please bring healing to the troubled land of Afghanistan. May You soften people's hearts and cause them to surrender their swords as they submit to the Prince of Peace. Thank You that You have Your people in this country. Strengthen them to persevere and help them cling to their Saviour. Lord, defend Your people and Your cause! I pray that Your kingdom might come soon among the Dari, Pashto and Turkmen people who reside here, no matter who claims to rule the nation.

DAY 7

AFGHANISTAN

Part 2

Your next day begins at a primary school in a poor quarter of Kabul. Outside the building, you meet a man named Darman who will be your guide. Years of war have hit education hard. The children are too young to remember the previous Taliban regime, so until recently this school had been generating hope for a better national future.

The modest-looking building is a far cry from what had existed before. Sixty girls were being educated here at one point but now only boys may attend. You enter a classroom where a boy of about eight is sat nearest to you. He wears clean clothes and sports a delighted smile having answered the teacher's question by holding up a bright-blue plastic 'B'. The class laugh and plead to be asked a question next. What an opportunity for them to learn English as well as their own language! Later, as you travel west, you reflect dejectedly on the different life opportunities for these children compared to those in the West. Many children, girls in particular, are unable to access an education in Kabul.

Your day ends with meeting a team working to help a group of young women. In this area, it is rare to meet a woman who can read and write. However, having lost their husbands, these mothers desperately need to support their children. You see them learning empowering vocational skills – cultivating seedlings, producing saffron, baking, growing mushrooms and much more. Through this project, the team has made connections with these women and with other local people, some of whom are secretly learning the truths of the Scriptures. The team pray that, through their practical efforts, hearts will be open to the One who meets our greatest need. For now, this work continues to fly under the radar of the authorities.

BIBLE VERSE

'... let your light shine before others, that they may see your good deeds and glorify your Father in heaven' (Mt. 5:16).

REFLECTION

Our good deeds are to be a light that shines before others, standing out from the darkness. They are to be seen by the world rather than hidden under a basket (vv. 14–15). While we are told to pray in secret where only the Father hears, we are to do good in public so that others will notice and remark upon it. Our public witness is the outcome of our faith. It is the visible representation of God's activity on earth today. And if our works are not seen, how will God's goodness be known? And if His goodness remains unknown, how will those who have never heard glorify God in heaven? Let's not fail to do all the good we can for all the people we can, wherever God may place us.

PRAYER

Lord, let the good deeds of Your people in Afghanistan shine brightly to all around them. May they shine like guiding stars in the dark to weary travellers. May those in Afghanistan who are secretly being drawn to the Saviour come to a firm faith and assurance. Please protect Your people and grow Your church. And help me too as I seek to honour You. Please draw many people to Yourself through the works You have prepared in advance for me to do.

DAY 8

KAZAKHSTAN

Part 1

Bordering Russia to the north, China to the south-east and several of the other '-stan' nations to the south, Kazakhstan is a much-forgotten country on the world stage. And so as you arrive in the capital city, commonly known as Astana, you are surprised to behold one of the most modern locations in Central Asia. Futuristic buildings lie at the feet of more conventional skyscrapers in the hub of Kazakhstan's politics, culture and commerce. As you explore the streets, you discover Western hotel chains, graceful glass-fronted museums and the jaw-dropping Baiterek Tower – an elegant structure whose 100-metre-high shafts support a golden sphere 22 metres in diameter.

You soon come across the name Nursultan Nazerbayev. Upon independence from Soviet rule in 1991, Nazerbayev become the nation's first president, and his vision for a prosperous, cosmopolitan future led to the city you are exploring today. Following a near 30-year tenure blighted by accusations of human rights violations, he resigned in 2019. However, the capital city was renamed after him following a unanimous vote in the nation's parliament. Today, the city is officially known as Nur-Sultan.

You notice a Russian influence here too, not only in restaurants and museums but also in the conversation around you. Alongside Kazakh, Russian remains a prominent language thanks to Soviet influence and migration, with Russian Orthodox immigrants representing the majority of the nation's Christians. Among the ethnic Kazakhs, just 0.1% have any form of Christian identity, and even less are active followers of Christ. The vast majority of the Kazakh people who walk by you do not know a Christian and will never have heard the claims of Jesus Christ. With so few believers among their own people, each Kazakh person has very little chance of hearing the gospel in their lifetime.

BIBLE VERSE

'You have rebuked the nations and destroyed the wicked; you have blotted out their name for ever and ever' (Ps. 9:5).

REFLECTION

For decades, religious belief and practice was suppressed not only in Kazakhstan but across the Soviet Union. The Bible depicts a long history of superpowers emerging (particularly the Babylonians and Assyrians in the Old Testament, and the Romans in the day of Jesus), who either restrict religious activity or impose their own cultural and religious practices on others. However, none of those powers exist today; nor does the Soviet Union. In Psalm 9, God intervened as the nations were persecuting David, His chosen king (v. 13). It can be disheartening to see the good news of Jesus, God's chosen King, opposed even today. However, we must take heart that God is sovereign. In His good timing, He acts in justice to topple those who stand against His purposes.

PRAYER

Lord, please help me to follow David's example, giving You thanks with all of my heart, telling of Your wondrous deeds and singing Your praise! Thank You that people in Kazakhstan now have the freedom to practise their religion. As so many Kazakhs have never heard the gospel, please raise up workers who speak their language and can take this wonderful message to them. I pray that many souls would be saved, that the church would grow and that You would be exalted in Kazakhstan.

DAY 9

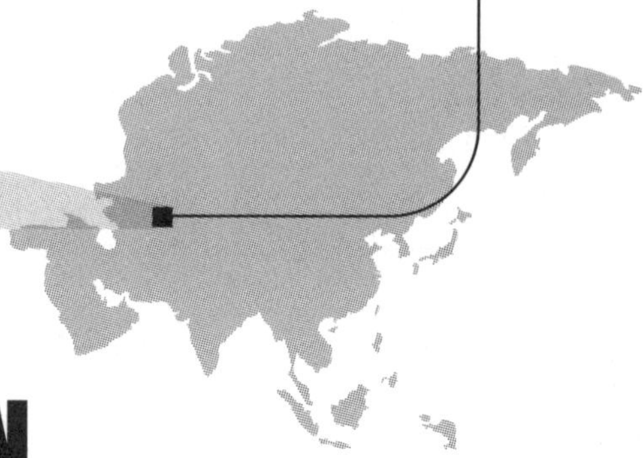

KAZAKHSTAN

Part 2

Beyond the capital city, this vast nation extends from the Caspian Sea in the west to the Altay mountains on the eastern border with China. For an authentic Kazakh experience, you travel to the south, where the traditional culture remains at its strongest. So vast and sparsely populated is this country that you drive for hours without the landscape ever seeming to change. As you travel long roads between distant cities, the vibrant green of endless rolling hills delights the eyes in the summer sun. You can only wonder how bleak and barren the scenery must be once the freezing winters roll in, with temperatures plummeting well below 0°C.

Several hours pass before you finally see signs of civilisation. Basic houses with tin roofs begin to line the streets before the vibrant buzz of urban life eventually surrounds you. Some locals busy themselves at market stalls, where the region's rich fruit and vegetable produce is on display, while others rest their legs in one of the many eateries. By the time you reach the town centre, Islamic shrines and places of worship become increasingly common, and you sense how central they are to Kazakh culture.

The nation's independence, following the dissolution of the Soviet Union, provided the opportunity for people to explore new ideas. As the suppression of religion came to an end, missionary activity and outreach from local churches gathered apace. There followed a period in which small numbers of Kazakhs were slowly and steadily being won for Christ. However, as the traditional nomadic way of life was all but eradicated in the Soviet era, the greatest trend for Kazakhs seeking a sense of cultural identity is a return to their historic Islamic traditions.

BIBLE VERSE

'Some of the people became followers of Paul and believed' (Acts 17:34).

REFLECTION

Imagine being one of the first missionaries in Kazakhstan following independence, sowing seeds in a field which had been cordoned off to Christ for almost a century! Imagine being in a local church whose numbers gradually swelled as faithful believers explained the gospel to their friends, family and neighbours. But then the growth slowed as more and more people rooted their identity in the culture and teachings of Islam. Was this an opportunity missed? Did the church get it wrong? Paul and the other apostles had many evangelistic successes. However, Acts 17 is one of numerous examples where they also faced rejection, with some of the Athenians sneering at Paul's claim that Jesus died and rose again (v. 32). We can wonder what might have been in Kazakhstan, or we can give thanks that the church stepped out in faith and that by God's grace some were saved.

PRAYER

Gracious God, thank You that Kazakhstan's independence brought freedom of worship and opened doors for the gospel. Thank You that missionaries and local believers were willing to share the gospel with those around them, and for every soul that was saved by the gracious work of Your Holy Spirit. Please continue to work in Kazakhstan, bringing more people to Yourself and building the church up in knowledge, wisdom and love. I pray that You would help me to step out in faith and share the gospel too, even though I may face rejection.

DAY 10

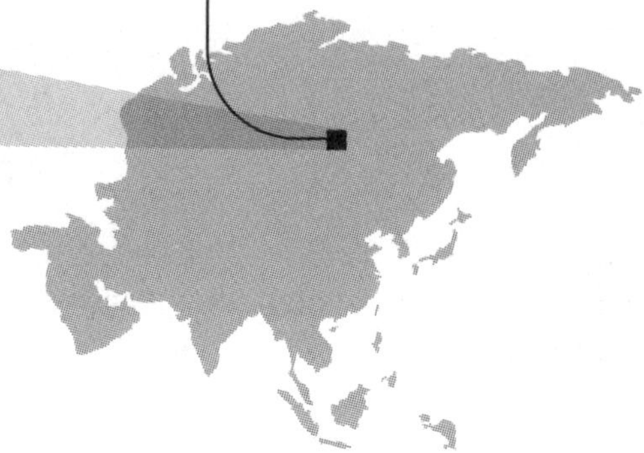

MONGOLIA

Part 1

The naming of Mongolia's international airport after Genghis Khan is a reminder of this nation's rich heritage, having once been the centre of the most powerful empire in history. With Genghis Khan the most successful and, arguably, most ruthless military leader of all time, the Mongol Empire encompassed large swathes of Asia under his leadership. However, as you step out of the airport today, you quickly realise that those days of wealth, power and influence are long gone.

The drab, grey buildings on the outskirts of Ulaanbaatar have that distinctive Soviet look – a tell-tale sign of the communist rule which lasted much of the 20th century. In the city centre sits the impressive Sukhbaatar Square, named after the leader who was instrumental in the socialist revolution of 1921. Almost 70 years later, the square took centre stage again when a peaceful protest saw over 100,000 people gather to call for democracy. Since independence in 1990, futuristic, high-rise office buildings have sprouted up around the square. However, as you explore the side streets, the dull, featureless architecture continues to reflect the utilitarian Soviet era. Every now and then, the beautifully ornate shape of a Buddhist temple appears, in stark contrast to the angular, grey surroundings.

Escaping the congested streets of the city, it's not long before you understand why Mongolia is the most sparsely populated country in the world. Wide rolling countryside spreads to the horizon with no buildings or civilization in sight. The nomadic lifestyle, a means of survival and livelihood here for generations, is being abandoned as extreme poverty and harsh winter temperatures drive the population into towns and cities. The spiritual landscape is changing too, with the darkness of cultural Buddhism and traditional folk religion being slowly challenged and transformed by the light of the gospel.

BIBLE VERSE

'The desert and the parched land will be glad; the wilderness will rejoice and blossom'
(Is. 35:1).

REFLECTION

The Mongolian grasslands strike you as one of the most barren and inhospitable places you can imagine. Further south, where Mongolia borders China, the Gobi Desert stretches for miles and the mind boggles that anything could possibly grow there. In Isaiah 35, the prophet paints a similar picture to describe Israel's spiritual climate. He uses images such as wild pastureland, bare moors and sandy grasslands. This reflects much of Mongolia's history, not only geographically but also spiritually – a barren wilderness. If we're honest, searching our own hearts at times reveals a similar picture of dearth and barrenness. Yet as Isaiah 35 goes on to offer great hope to Israel, we too can blossom and flourish as we draw upon Christ's lifegiving streams. May that also become the experience of many people in Mongolia!

PRAYER

Heavenly Father, thank You that all I need for life and fruitfulness is found in You. In times when I feel spiritually empty and dry, teach me to draw fresh strength and vitality from You. Lord, please move in my own nation and pour out Your Spirit so that we may experience a season of refreshing in our church. I pray for the country of Mongolia too – may Your blessing fall on the growing church there, so that it might flourish and be fruitful, growing both in depth and breadth in the life of Christ.

DAY 11

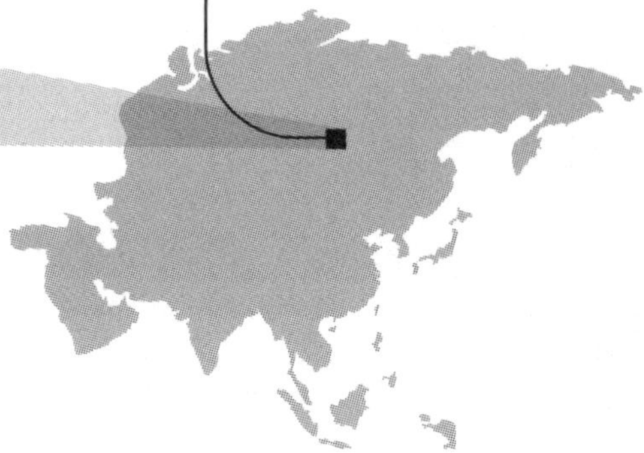

MONGOLIA

Part 2

You travel north, thankful for the helpful tip to reserve a seat on the shaded side of the bus. Across the aisle, an elderly couple in traditional Mongolian dress are sweltering as the sun glares in. Not that your side is much more pleasant, with no air conditioning, seven hours of bumpy roads and a Mongolian *X Factor* video playing on repeat. At the halfway comfort stop, you discover that 'comfort' is a relative term. After a quick visit to a foul-smelling, rickety shack, you're glad to be on the road again!

Several hours in, you realise there have been no buildings – only a few gers dotted here and there. When you finally arrive in Erdenet, a warm-hearted couple take you to their small Bible school where the first post-Soviet missionaries saw amazing things happen in the early 1990s. There were four believers in Mongolia in 1989; now the church numbers tens of thousands. As you enter, a banner reads: 'Our vision is to plant a church in every town in Mongolia and to evangelise the entire former Mongol Empire.' A map on the wall depicts the unreached settlements with hundreds of red dots, and you admire their ambition!

The corridor is busy with students sweeping, tidying and preparing food. Chatting with students later, you learn that many have made great sacrifices to be here. Often, their families disown them as they pursue God's plan for their lives, studying God's Word in preparation to become pastors, evangelists and church planters. The highlight of the visit is joining with staff and students for worship and devotions. This significant place in the Mongolian church-planting movement has shown you once again the greatness of God.

BIBLE VERSE

'Do your best to present yourself to God as one approved, a worker who does not need to be ashamed and who correctly handles the word of truth'
(2 Tim. 2:15).

REFLECTION

The church in Mongolia has grown at a phenomenal rate since the early 1990s. As a young church with many first-generation believers, sound Bible teaching is crucial. You may have heard the expression that it's possible for something to be 'a mile wide but just an inch deep'. What a great opportunity we have to encourage and support the training of future pastors and evangelists, ensuring that the church in Mongolia continues to grow wide in influence and deep in the Scriptures. As opportunities arise for you to witness to a friend, teach a children's lesson or serve in other ways, make sure you take the words of 2 Timothy 2:15 to heart and 'rightly handle the word of truth', just as the students in Mongolia and elsewhere are taught!

PRAYER

Thank You, Lord, for such amazing church growth in Mongolia. Thank You that the strongholds of communism are no match for Your Holy Spirit. I pray today for the Bible school in Erdenet – may the students and staff find rich blessing as they gather around Your Word. Please continue to raise up workers from that place who will serve the church in Mongolia, and please provide for their every need, both practically and spiritually. As students complete their studies, please give them all clear leading and direction in the next steps You have laid out for them.

DAY 12

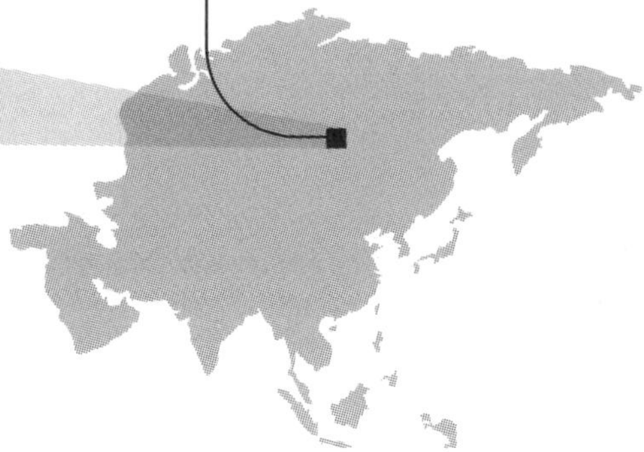

MONGOLIA

Part 3

It's another dry and sunny day back in the capital as you travel up Peace Avenue, Ulaanbaatar's main thoroughfare. Sometimes called the 'land of eternal blue sky', Mongolia enjoys lots of sunshine, even though winter temperatures regularly drop to a brutally cold -40°C or lower. Today, though, it's warm t-shirt weather and the city streets are dry and dusty.

You arrive at a small compound situated next to the city dump and stop for a closer look at the slum houses. Suddenly, a car pulls up and an angry man shouts what you assume are Mongolian obscenities before demanding to see the photos on your phone. He doesn't want the outside world to see that thousands of people live on the dump, scraping an existence by scavenging for recyclable materials. Missionaries who were serving in Mongolia in the early 1990s were heartbroken as they watched the carcass of a dead dog, lying among the rubbish, being carved up for food by the hungry residents. Moved with compassion, they started a feeding programme and began reaching out with the love of Christ. This was the beginning of the centre you are visiting today.

It is an emotional sight at lunchtime when the children gather and, after giving thanks, tuck into their lunch of buuz. You can only imagine the hopelessness these children face. Most will never go to school. Even early in their lives, they will encounter people who will try to exploit them. Some will develop respiratory issues as a result of the severe pollution and their life expectancy will be in the late 30s. Later in the afternoon, you leave the centre with a strong sense that the memory of these children will never leave you.

BIBLE VERSE

'Lord, when did we see you hungry and feed you, or thirsty and give you something to drink?'
(Mt. 25:37).

REFLECTION

Many of Jesus' hearers couldn't understand that, on a daily basis, they had overlooked opportunities to minister to Him. Jesus exposed their failure to respond to the hunger, poverty and injustice around them. Those living on the dump in Ulaanbaatar are human beings like you and me, made in the image of God with value, worth and dignity. Yet their poverty means their lives can look more similar to those of rodents, burrowing into the rubbish and scurrying about to find food. The centre here is offering hope to children and young people who otherwise face nothing but this degradation, hopelessness and despair. Alongside the practical help offered, the team are also ministering God's Word into their lives. Wonderfully, several have trusted Christ and found real hope in Him.

PRAYER

Lord, thank You for the missionary vision of this centre in Mongolia. I pray that the team would be strengthened to serve You in this very challenging setting. Day by day, may they be motivated and driven by Your love. Please give them the wonderful joy of seeing many children and their families come to Christ. Lord, forgive me for often being blind to the needs around me, both here at home and in places like Mongolia. Help me to see as You see, to be moved with compassion and to respond in whatever way I can.

DAY 13

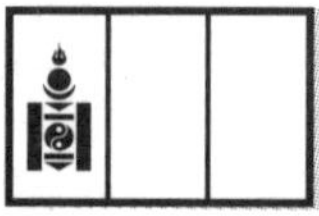

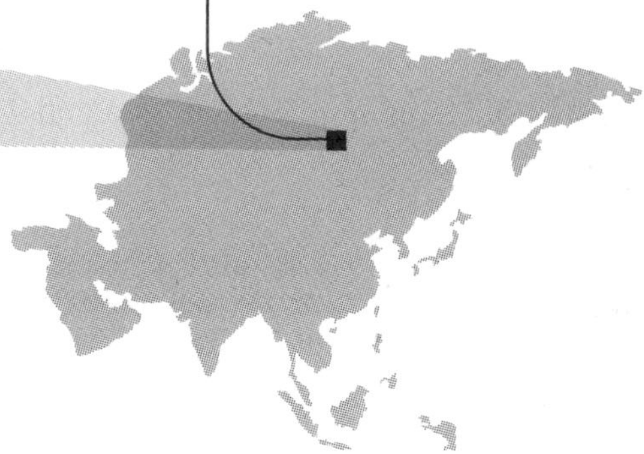

MONGOLIA

Part 4

You have seen countless traditional gers while travelling around over the past few days – some dotted around the countryside but whole districts of them in the city. Today, however, you look forward to seeing one from the inside.

On the edge of Mongolia's towns and cities, ger districts accommodate many of the poorer families. You pick your way over very rough terrain – there are no proper roads – as you weave between gers and other makeshift dwellings. A young, nervous-looking girl stands at the door of one ger where she lives with her mother, father and little brother. Her name is Savlaigul. You notice that her body language is awkward in the presence of her father and sense that this is not a happy home. Alcohol is a major factor in domestic abuse in Mongolia, with vodka selling for half the price of bottled water. You cannot help but wonder, ruefully, if this is affecting the family before you.

You remove your shoes and stoop to enter the circular tent before examining how it is put together. Bright, colourful fabric hangs down from the wooden trellis sides while roof timbers reach up to support the domed roof. A stove sits in the centre. Although it is comfortably warm today, you imagine the nightmare of living here through the wintertime. Savlaigul tells you of the day she received a winter kit, including boots and a coat. They have made the hour-long walk to school possible throughout the winter, enabling her to carry on learning and to attend life skills classes. You lean forward and ask, 'What else did you get with your winter kit?' Savlaigul's answer blows you away as she responds, 'I heard about Jesus.'

BIBLE VERSE

'I delight greatly in the Lord; my soul rejoices in my God. For he has clothed me with garments of salvation and arrayed me in a robe of his righteousness'
(Is. 61:10).

REFLECTION

Winter kits have been a great help to many poor families in Mongolia. Through this very practical ministry, believers have also been given great opportunities to share the gospel. We all have an obligation to reach out to the needy and destitute in this way, yet it is always good to remember the most loving thing we can do for anyone: to tell them of the God who loves them and sent His Son to die on the cross for them. We must take to heart the truth Isaiah gives us that being clothed in the garments of salvation means everything. Through the grace and mercy of God, Savlaigul and some of her family placed their trust in Christ as their Saviour. They now attend a local church and are growing in their faith.

PRAYER

Loving Father, please bless Savlaigul, her family and others like them today. Please watch over and protect them, and help them to grow in their walk with You. Continue to use believers as they provide poor families with winter kits and give them opportunities to share the gospel. I pray for the many sad and hurting homes in Mongolia. Lord, please move in the power of Your Holy Spirit so that many more people might be comforted, healed and clothed in the righteousness of Christ.

DAY 14

MONGOLIA

Part 5

In Mongolia, like everywhere else subsumed by Soviet communism, large heating pipes run alongside the roads, carrying hot water around the city from coal-fired power stations. As well as heating whole swathes of apartment blocks, these pipes also create a network of warm tunnels beneath the ground. In the harsh winters, a community nicknamed 'the ant people' live in these tunnels and underground dens. There is nobody down there on this warm summer's day, but with many manhole covers cracked or missing, it is easy to look down and see these places. Traffickers often target this community, many of whom struggle with drug and alcohol addictions and are lured into prostitution as a way out of hardship and poverty.

You visit a safehouse and training workshop where women rescued from such exploitation are given a new start. The building is quite discreet, with no sign of the work which takes place within. Once inside, the gracious man who directs the ministry tells you, 'Feel free to take pictures and video, but no faces.' He is keen to protect the dignity of these women.

The backgrounds of the women here are heartbreaking. One had been reached by the team here and rescued from a life of prostitution, only to be pursued by her former pimp. A series of attacks followed. Her head was split open with a hatchet. She was also chased out in front of a car and suffered a broken leg and other injuries. Thankfully, she is now in this safe place, learning a new skill and studying God's Word every day.

BIBLE VERSE

'He lifted me out of the slimy pit, out of the mud and mire; he set my feet on a rock and gave me a firm place to stand' (Ps. 40:2).

REFLECTION

This testimony of David paints a vivid picture of what it is to feel lost and helpless. Perhaps this language came from a personal experience, either of David being rescued from a pit himself or instead being the rescuer of a sheep which had fallen. Either way, the spiritual parallels are clear! While you may never have spiralled into such destructive lifestyles as some of the women you met today, we all have countless reasons to give thanks for Christ our Rescuer. The psalm reminds us that we can find help and security even in those first steps as we establish a sure footing on the Rock. Those working among exploited women face many challenges: the work is slow and there are many setbacks. Yet their love for and commitment to the women they reach is amazing. Many broken lives are being wonderfully transformed by the power of the gospel!

PRAYER

Dear Lord, I pray that You would give great resilience and spiritual wisdom to those who lead ministries among exploited women. As they take to the streets to engage with women, please break down barriers and bless their conversations. Help those in the safe house in Mongolia to see the love of God in action day by day. I ask that many more women would come to know Christ their Rescuer. Please help them to find security and strength as they take the first steps in their new life with Him.

DAY 15

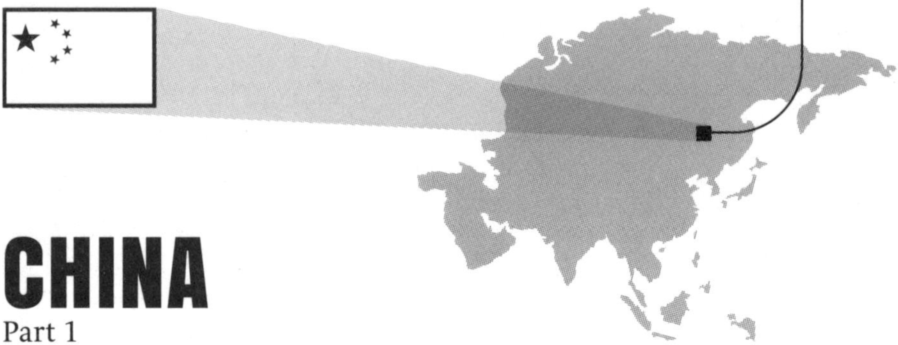

CHINA
Part 1

As you make your way by taxi into the city of Beijing, you are surprised by how lush and well-manicured the roadsides seem to be. You shift slightly nervously in your seat as the vehicle weaves between several lanes of traffic and wonder how you will make the rest of your journey without a bump or a scrape. Your driver speaks little English and the conversation soon dries up, leaving you alone with your thoughts.

On either side of the road stand high-rise apartment blocks. A few are white with vertical pink stripes; others a dull red. These functional giants are the result of Beijing's 20 million souls needing to be housed. You imagine countless similar blocks across numerous other cities to accommodate the nation's population of 1.3 billion. You pass silver office towers and glass-fronted skyscrapers which dwarf the trees below. Beyond, in the grey, hazy distance, still others are under construction, hemmed in by watchful cranes. China boasts the world's fastest-growing major economy, as evidenced by the modern buildings and distant developments before you.

As you near the city, with traffic building, a car horn whining and the taxi slowing, evidence of China's ancient past appears. You have time to savour a double-roofed temple, perhaps 500 years old, bearing its mute testimony of a bygone age to the commuters of modern Beijing. The eaves curve upwards at each corner to ward off evil spirits who, this officially atheist nation still believes, can only travel in straight lines. As you arrive at your hotel, you ponder the fact that China has changed so much – and yet perhaps little has really changed.

BIBLE VERSE

'Jesus answered, "It is written: 'Man shall not live on bread alone, but on every word that comes from the mouth of God'"' (Mt. 4:4).

REFLECTION

There is no doubt that much good has come from China's progress from poverty, for which we can be grateful. Of course, many still live in what most westerners would describe as serious deprivation, but have been delivered from a hand-to-mouth existence. However, the official doctrine of the ruling Communist Party doesn't acknowledge that there is an even more important realm than the material. In Scripture, humans are indeed made from dust and in need of daily bread. And yet we are gloriously the image of God too: made for fellowship with and reliance upon our Creator. Our physical hunger is paralleled with our spiritual hunger. We need God's Word to have life in the fullest sense.

PRAYER

Lord, thank You for meeting my material needs. Thank You that You are not only the maker of my flesh but my sustainer too. And thank You for sustaining my spiritual needs through the bread of heaven, the Lord Jesus. It is through Your living and active Word that we come to spiritual life. In Your mercy, please help the people of China to see that their deepest longings for life and true prosperity are met in Jesus.

DAY 16

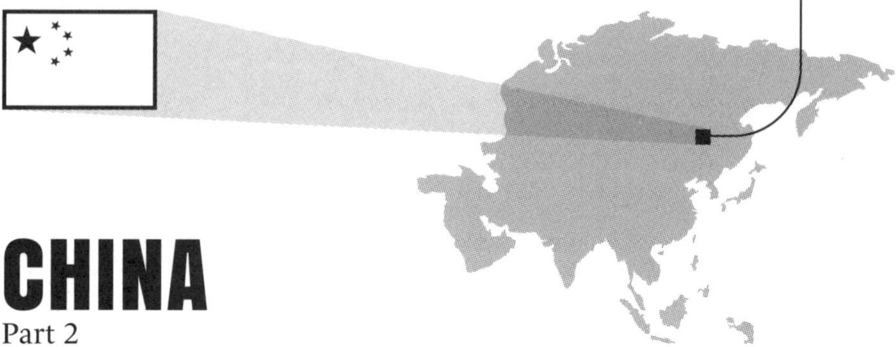

CHINA

Part 2

You meet for lunch with a Chinese Christian who explains what it's like to be a believer in the new China. 'The authorities are quite worried about the growth of the church in China,' he explains. 'They want to stop young people believing, so we cannot allow young people into Sunday school.' His sentence trails off as the waiter comes to the table bringing more dishes and tea. You eat some more rice, quietly pleased with your own progress in using chopsticks! 'Last year,' he continues quietly, 'churches in Henan province in the south had to replace their Ten Commandments with a picture of the president. It's getting very difficult because churches can't rent buildings unless they are registered. And if we register, they try to control us more. But you can't control the Holy Spirit,' he smiles.

Church leaders say that persecution is reaching levels not seen since the 60s and 70s. Despite the pressure, the church has grown too. One researcher claims there are 120 million Bible-believing followers of Jesus. 'When the missionaries were thrown out in 1949, do you think God's presence left with them?' your friend asks. You wonder if your faith matches his. And what will happen when the Christians are deemed not to have enough 'social credit'? Will they be 're-educated' like some of the Uyghur Muslims in the far west of China?

Later, you drive past an empty block where a church once stood. It was raided in December 2018, then shut down and demolished. Why? Their pastor refused to install CCTV cameras to provide live footage of services to the authorities.

BIBLE VERSE

'But rejoice inasmuch as you participate in the sufferings of Christ, so that you may be overjoyed when his glory is revealed' (1 Pet. 4:13).

REFLECTION

The church faces pressure everywhere it grows, and this is especially true in China. This is to be expected. Jesus said, 'If the world hates you, keep in mind that it hated me first' (John 15:18). So we are not surprised at any ordeal that comes to test us, 'as though something strange were happening' (1 Pet. 4:12). Rather, we rejoice along with all who share in Christ's sufferings. Why? Because He who suffered for us was raised to glory that we might also share in His glory. There are no shortcuts to the celestial city. The path is not flower-strewn and there is no crown without a cross. And yet on this road we are accompanied by One who promises never to leave or forsake us, giving us a peace beyond understanding as we continue the journey. With every step, we remember the glory that will one day be revealed.

PRAYER

Father, help me to learn from those brothers and sisters in China who rejoice in their sufferings. Help me to learn what it is to rejoice through suffering in the hope of future glory. Please protect Your church in China and cause her to grow even more, preventing worldly powers from standing against the working of Your Spirit. Help Your people to be bold and forgiving, wise and godly. For those in prison, please encourage them to remain strong in faith, and keep the light of hope illuminated in their hearts.

DAY 17

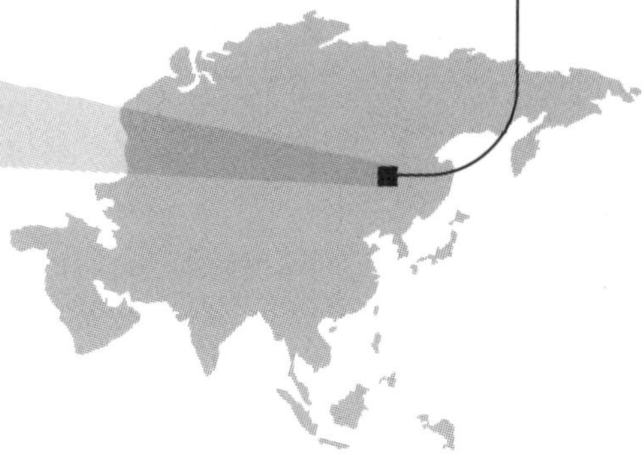

CHINA

Part 3

Today, you join a team delivering Bibles to a rural house church. Chinese Bibles can be mass produced for less than two dollars each, but while many Bibles are printed here, most are exported. Very few reach local churches, and the government has even begun editing Scripture to include its own propaganda. With thousands of believers being added to the church each day, there is an insatiable need for the true Word of God. The group you have joined distribute thousands of Bibles every month through the churches, but many believers still have no Bible, including those before you today.

Inside a plain room, suitcases are opened to reveal precious cargo. A whoop of delight is followed by excited voices, like young children playing games at a party. There is an eager rush as each of the 20 people takes their first copy of God's Word. A young man bends his head and kisses the book several times, a hint of a tear in his eyes. A lady nearby looks at the cover and is also kissing the book, lost for words and trying to take it all in. Another woman smiles and shares her delight with a friend as she tears off the wrapping, before opening the pages and reading a few lines to herself.

A lady stands up and speaks, as if for them all. Somebody translates, explaining that she is committing herself to reading God's Word every day and living by its teaching. The mood has turned quite sombre as a few sob quietly. The group take turns to pray, passionately giving thanks for the goodness of God in meeting this desire long held in their hearts. What a privilege to witness this scene!

BIBLE VERSE

'The law from your mouth is more precious to me than thousands of pieces of silver and gold' (Ps. 119:72).

REFLECTION

When the natives of one of the islands of Vanuatu believed the gospel, they desired their missionary friend, John Paton, to have the Bible translated and printed in their own language. But the cost was £1200, a vast sum to these poor islanders in the 19th century. Still, they agreed to work and export their crop until this amount was raised. It took 15 long years of toil under a tropical sun, but they agreed with the psalmist that God's Word is more valuable than gold and silver. We often take for granted our immediate access to the Word of God in our own language. But we must never forget that it is the source of wisdom which leads to eternal life. It cannot be exchanged for jewels or precious stones because it points to Him who is more precious than rubies: the Lord Jesus Himself!

PRAYER

Lord, please help Your church to provide every Chinese Christian with a Bible in their heart language. Let Bibles be printed and distributed throughout this vast land, and enable these believers also to have safe access to Scripture through technology. Lord, please cause the authorities to relax restrictions on the production, distribution and possession of Scripture. May they see that Your Word is indeed sweeter than honey and more valuable than gold and silver. Help me to treasure Your Word and be grateful for those who have translated it and made it available.

DAY 18

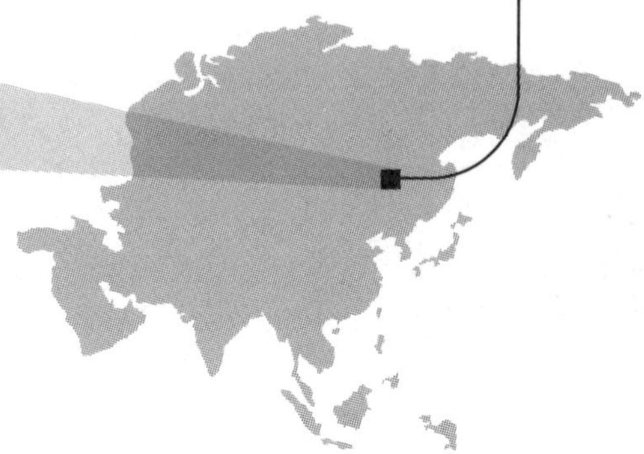

CHINA

Part 4

You hand an address to a taxi driver as you hesitantly enter his vehicle, and pray you'll end up in the right place. Thankfully, as he drops you off at a high-rise block of flats outside the city centre, you recognise it from the pictures you saw online. The security guard directs you to the 18th floor, where you're greeted by a short, thin man with dark hair. His English is reasonable – strong enough to sustain a conversation.

His name is Li Jun. He was arrested a few years ago for sharing the gospel and was beaten so badly that he almost died. He pours tea while his young daughter plays on the floor nearby. You can't help but notice that he moves slowly for a man still in the prime of life.

'Some evangelists are arrested and never seen again. They are treated like criminals. But the power of God cannot be stopped, even by the government.' He smiles, but not too broadly. He is serious and not prone to too many moments of levity. You point out that the Chinese constitution guarantees freedom of faith. 'Oh yes,' he replies, 'but there are other regulations. The church must be registered. Its message must support the government. The government says what we must do.'

Li Jun goes onto explain that it is difficult to find work now. His bad back makes it hard to stand for a long time and so the need to earn an income hangs over him. However, he tells you that he receives support from Christians elsewhere in the world. They call him a 'living martyr' after he suffered so badly for his faith. Without help, this man would struggle to provide for his daughter and wife.

BIBLE VERSE

'Share with the Lord's people who are in need' (Rom. 12:13).

REFLECTION

For love to be sincere, it must reject evil, cling to what is good and be devoted to the good of others (v. 9). The first Christians were encouraged to show such love by contributing towards the needs of fellow believers, entering into and helping with their troubles. The life of the Christian cannot be reduced to an internal, personal level. Rather, we are called to see ourselves as a body united in Christ, connecting us to all its members around the world. If one part is hurting, then the whole body hurts. If one part lacks, the whole body does too. If a man cannot support his family because of what he suffered for Christ, then he has a need. And that is where the body has the opportunity, duty and privilege to contribute.

PRAYER

Lord, thank You for those who have the courage to share the gospel in countries where open proclamation of the gospel is costly. Please strengthen and encourage those who have been incapacitated through ill treatment. For the widows and orphans of martyrs, I pray that their needs would be met through Your body, the church. Please open my heart and the heart of Your global church to be agents through whom such help might come. Please give me eyes to see needs around me, along with a heart which cares and hands which are ready to serve.

DAY 19

NORTH KOREA

Part 1

You come out of the consulate of the Democratic People's Republic of Korea in Shenyang, China and look at the visa in your passport. Only now do you realise that it is true – you are really going to North Korea, the graveyard of Christians and still among the most dangerous places in the world to follow Jesus.

Sitting in the departure lounge of the airport, you look out of the window across the airfield. A white Russian Tupelov aircraft, which could be over 20 years old, features a single red stripe embellished with the words 'Air Koryo'. You wonder if this machine will ever get off the ground – a feeling only enhanced by the significant, unexplained delay after boarding. Once your journey begins, the first thing that strikes you is the fact that no one on the aircraft speaks anything other than Korean. South or north, it is the same language. That is of little concern, though – the journey time is less than an hour. You take the time to look at the magazine with its glossy pictures of tractors and industrial power, and quickly realise that the barrage of propaganda has begun. You are not yet in the country.

Arriving in Pyongyang International Airport is an experience in itself – there is a lack of aircraft as Air Koryo only serves four international destinations. As you make your way to immigration and customs, you also notice the absolute glut of military uniforms – all brown – and the near silence, broken only by the luggage belts whirring their international song. None of the staff speak to you and there is no eye contact. It is cold, clinical and very off-putting. Welcome to North Korea.

BIBLE VERSE

'Be strong and courageous. Do not be afraid or terrified because of them, for the Lord your God goes with you; he will never leave you nor forsake you'
(Deut. 31:6).

REFLECTION

Ever since the beginning of the North Korean regime on 9 September 1948, the people have been told that there is no God and that the state and its leaders in particular assume the mantle of God. The evidence of that is clear, even in the midst of an airport: the coldness; the images of the former leaders; the distance that people maintain from one another; and the seeming lack of social awareness. It can be scary and totally off-putting. As you look at the people and the sadness in their eyes, you remember that God may be denied but He cannot be eradicated. You look and you love because your heart breaks. At times like this, we must take heart in the truth that Christ lives in us by His Spirit. He is with us always. You are not forsaken – and neither are these people of North Korea.

PRAYER

Thank You, Lord God Almighty, that though Your very existence is often denied, this is still Your world and You reveal Yourself to those who will seek You. Thank You that we can see Your handiwork in creation and Your image in one another. Please break through the lies and make Yourself known to the broken and impoverished people of North Korea.

DAY 20

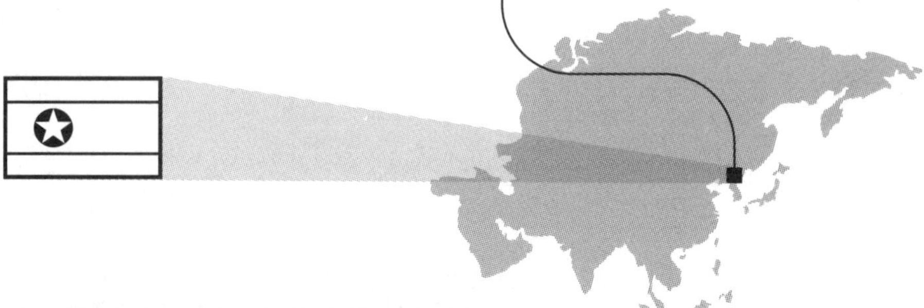

NORTH KOREA

Part 2

You are ready to leave Pyongyang International Airport and keen to see what this city and the country have to offer. However, before you set foot on the pavement outside the terminal building, you are greeted by your government 'guides', better described as minders. They will be with you everywhere you go, regulating what you see and what you can photograph and film. One of them, Kim, speaks excellent English and seems so friendly you almost get the feeling she is glad to see you. The other gives a different impression altogether!

Exiting the airport, you are struck by the fact that the main highway into the city has so few cars, or any other vehicles for that matter. You move along steadily, taking in the sights and hoping that your guide does not see you taking pictures out of the window. High-rise flats punctuate the journey as you approach the centre of the city. They are painted green, red and blue, but the colours only magnify the poverty as the paint flakes and peels from the walls.

The city surprises you in so many ways. The women are dressed in dark colours and almost all wear dresses or skirts. Those men not in military attire wear the civilian uniform of dark trousers and a white shirt, many with scarlet neckerchiefs. Then there are military uniforms everywhere and in great number, with some soldiers carrying rifles. And the military hats are huge! Do all North Korean men have such large heads? There are bicycles as far as the eye can see, with everyone else walking. So many of them, and not a smile in sight. It is almost as if the whole people are in mourning. You wonder if any of them have ever heard of Jesus.

BIBLE VERSE

'So God created mankind in his own image, in the image of God he created them; male and female he created them' (Gen. 1:27).

REFLECTION

When you go to North Korea, it can be so easy to get caught up in thinking about the regime and its paraphernalia which surrounds you on every side, as well as the real and brutal persecution of Christians. But the whole point of ministry in this country is for the people. It is important to take time to look past the sadness and the sense of resignation, and to see the image of God; to remind yourself that these are those for whom Christ died; and to seek, by the power of God's Spirit, to show the love of Christ. Jesus came to seek and to save the lost, and in North Korea you get an overwhelming sense of that lostness.

PRAYER

God Almighty, You call us to lift our eyes off systems, regimes and politics, and to look at lost people. Please help me to see the North Koreans as You see them – as sheep who have no shepherd. Remind me that they are created, as I am, in Your image, and that these are those for whom Christ died. Please energise me in my prayers, and others too, that we might be able to see a spiritual revolution as the light of Christ penetrates the spiritual darkness in North Korea.

DAY 21

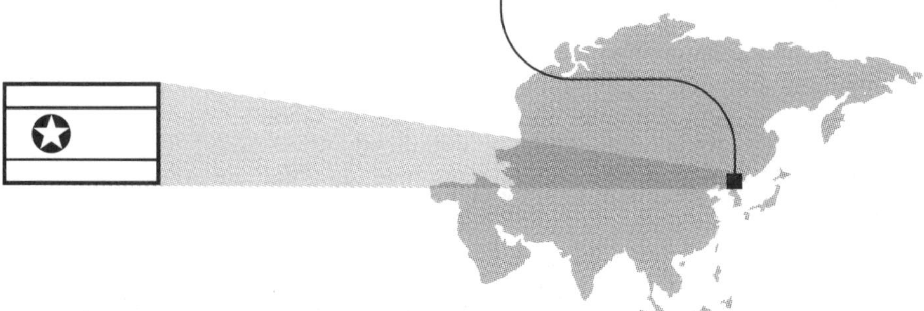

NORTH KOREA

Part 3

Arriving at the orphanage which 200 pre-school-aged children call home is truly humbling. However, what you first notice, even before meeting the children, are the images of Kim Il Sung, the founder of modern North Korea, and his son, Kim Jong Il. Their pictures are everywhere – above the entrance, on almost every wall in the building and in all of the children's rooms.

Han is the manager, and she welcomes you with a smile and food. 'You have come to see the next group of children ready for the cleft lip surgery?' As the children are brought in, you draw breath – you have never seen so many children with cleft lips in one place. The children are obviously well cared for, yet the look on their faces is one of sadness. Later, in a nearby hospital, you meet some families whose children have also had the surgery, and are encouraged by the smiles on the faces of mothers and children alike. To give a smile back to a child is a precious gift! The look of joy and amazement on their faces as you share your Polo mints reminds you that showing the love of Jesus is a powerful act, even though you also long to tell each of them about His love.

Names are not shared but it does not seem important. Knowing that even a cup of water given in the name of Jesus blesses His heart makes your journey so very worthwhile, despite travelling 150 kilometres on roads seemingly unchanged since the bombings of the Korean War in 1953. You might not be able to preach the gospel without facing imprisonment or even worse in this Hermit Kingdom, but you can still love in the name of Jesus and pray for those you meet.

BIBLE VERSE

'Dear children, let us not love with words or speech but with actions and in truth'
(1 John 3:18).

REFLECTION

While the specific context of John's instruction relates to loving the people of God, love in action must surely include those who do not know Jesus. As such, 1 John 3:16–18 form a helpful model for our outreach where verbal proclamation is restricted. In North Korea, just the mention of Jesus' name puts you in very real danger, along with anyone with whom you might want to share the gospel. Here, it can be hard to communicate the fact that God loves the people and wants them to know Him through Jesus, His only begotten Son. In this situation, communicating God's love relies on His people showing love to alleviate the suffering of these children. This love is a powerful expression of God's own loving nature and honours the One who laid down His life for us.

PRAYER

Gracious God, thank You that the Lord Jesus came not just to speak of the love of His Father but to show it. Thank You that He was not distant but intimate, and that those whom He met were left in no doubt as to His heart for them. Please let the children who receive this care, along with their families, experience the joy of being loved by You. Please help them to find the hope which is in Christ Jesus our Lord, even though it is so hard for believers to speak of You.

DAY 22

NORTH KOREA

Part 4

Nothing prepares you for the sight of squalor and the smell of poverty as you alight from the van and walk towards the school building. The children who study and live here are deaf and are hidden away from the eyes of mainstream society. You are met politely, with a smile and food, by the principal. His name is not given, nor yours requested, and you cannot help but be taken aback by his militaristic uniform. You are taken on a tour – the school is sparsely furnished and would be condemned in the West. You hear the children being taught, and listen as they seek to vocalise what they are being shown. Their poverty is visible in their appearance, their clothes basic. The outfits are modelled on military uniforms but are at least blue and white as opposed to dull brown. Some have not seen their families in months and their living conditions make you want to weep.

After the tour, you visit the huge greenhouses, filled with food. Your heart is gladdened that the North Korean authorities who run the school allowed foreign Christians to build these structures. It has not escaped your attention that the children in this nation are undernourished, making them significantly lighter and smaller than their South Korean neighbours. Strategies for future provision are discussed. The conversation is polite and formal, at times bordering on warmth, but you remain unsure whether or not you are trusted. This is ministry, but not as we know it.

The journey back to Pyongyang is quiet as you try to take in all that you have seen, heard and smelled. While the children's basic needs are taken care of, everything seems so cold, dispassionate and unloving. You just wish that you had been able to hug them.

BIBLE VERSE

'Jesus said, "Let the little children come to me, and do not hinder them, for the kingdom of heaven belongs to such as these"' (Mt. 19:14).

REFLECTION

In our society, children are largely well cared for and loved. Those who are disabled in some way are not hidden away so that we don't have to look on them, as though our sensibilities would be affected. Jesus showed us not only that children are to be valued but that, in some mysterious way, the kingdom of God belongs to them. Those who are the most vulnerable in our society surely deserve the greatest care. This is what we see in Jesus. May God grant that it would also be seen in us.

PRAYER

Father God, You are loving and gracious, and You reveal to us a heart uncompromising in love. You show us, in Jesus, how to love in fullness and in grace. Thank You that these children are fully loved by You and by those who seek to embrace them in the name of Jesus. Please help those conducting this work not just to be efficient in the mechanics of ministry, but to do so in a way which demonstrates to the children that they are truly loved.

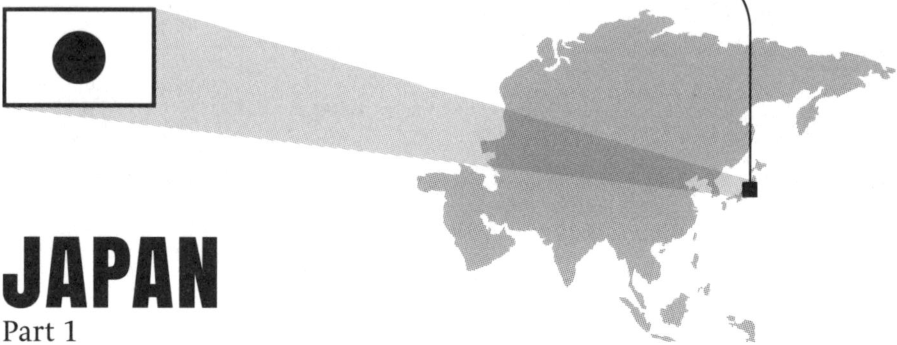

JAPAN

Part 1

Buses, taxis and trucks thunder down the busy streets of Tokyo between towering concrete and glass structures. Some buildings are plain, others brightly decorated and creatively designed. Slipping into a bookstore, you explore the manga comic section – far larger than any back home. There are stories of love and hate, heroes and villains and epic adventures, but not of mercy, grace or forgiveness – concepts alien to Japan's culture of honour and shame.

A local man, Riku, introduces himself. He is intrigued to discover that you will be meeting believers here – he has never met a Japanese Christian. In contrast to many Asian countries, Japan allows churches to meet freely. However, Christianity is seen as a Western religion. 'It is interesting, but it is not ours,' Riku says, affirming that Buddhism and Shinto are the true religions of Japan. Although few of the younger generation take their family religion seriously, obligations to exercise religious ceremonies remain and they often inherit altars, idols and tombs. Anyone who turns away from these practices faces a real risk of disownment as shame is brought on the family. Here, harmonious relationships are far more sacred than truth.

These are not the only challenges believers face. Some struggle to attend church as Sunday is their employer's busiest day of the week. Meanwhile, the religious sphere is considered private and the working culture has no place for social conversation, making gospel witness a real challenge. Add to this the scarcity of faithful literature and the empty theological colleges and you begin to see why as few as 0.2% of Japanese people are committed followers of Jesus. There is much work to be done.

BIBLE VERSE

'... my only aim is to finish the race and complete the task the Lord Jesus has given me – the task of testifying to the good news of God's grace'
(Acts 20:24).

REFLECTION

The gospel message jars against some central elements of Japanese culture. Ideas of honour and shame stand in stark contrast to God's message of mercy and grace. The desire to maintain family harmony goes against Jesus' promise of rewards for those who leave houses, brothers, sisters, fathers, mothers, wives and children for His sake (Mt. 19:29). Nor does the Japanese language even have a word which suitably conveys the idea of sin, making gospel presentations a significant challenge. Nevertheless, the Lord is mighty to save. He knows the heart of every person in Japan and He will call those who belong to Him. Our response must be the same as Paul's – to finish the race and complete the task the Lord Jesus has given the church. One way or another, the people of Japan must hear the gospel (Acts 20:20–23).

PRAYER

Lord, thank You for bringing people into my life who shared the gospel with me, and for softening my heart to that glorious message. I pray for the people of Japan, who have grown up in a culture so opposed to this good news. Please break through the barriers of false religion, of honour and shame and of linguistic difficulties, so that the people of Japan might seek You while You may be found. Please help the church in Japan to be salt and light, set apart in a culture which has so little desire to know You.

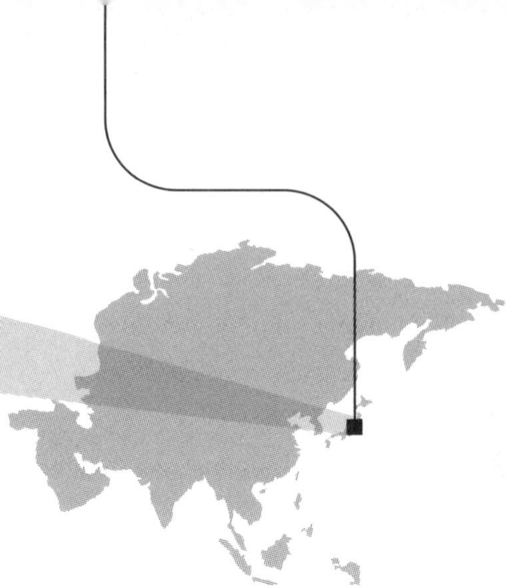

JAPAN

Part 2

Today, you are meeting several local believers in a sushi bar to learn more about the church in Japan. After taking their food recommendations, you ask about their experiences. Izumi speaks first, energetically describing a training course whose goal is to train 20–40 interns per year as they serve full-time in local churches. So far, 18 have taken the course. Some went on to plant churches or continue in their existing ministry, while others returned to the workplace to witness there.

Takahiro takes over. Older and more pensive than Izumi, he carefully explains more about office fellowship groups. These meet regularly in the mornings, at lunchtime or after work, either in a restaurant or in the office block itself. The key is for groups to be accessible to outsiders, with content varying to suit those attending. The lady to Takahiro's right is called Noriko and is in her mid-40s. She explains that she has been working in offices for 18 years and had never shared the gospel with her colleagues. However, after attending a lunchtime group, she felt encouraged to invite her colleagues out for coffee after work. Several people came along, and she then had the chance to invite one to the next lunchtime meeting. Noriko is praying that her colleague will turn up and be receptive to the gospel.

Finally, an older lady named Tamiko tells of her experience in the local church. She has been trying for years to get home groups up and running, despite meeting in people's homes and learning through discussion being quite counter-cultural. She is finally starting to see fruit but wonders whether these groups would continue without her. Her greatest concern is who will lead Japan's churches with so few believers among the next generation.

BIBLE VERSE

'... we will tell the next generation the praiseworthy deeds of the L*ORD'*
(Ps. 78:4).

REFLECTION

With so few believers in Japan, it is encouraging to hear that training ministries, office outreaches and home groups are beginning to take place. However, the church in this nation remains fragile, with few leaders being prepared for the task of taking the church forward as the Spirit leads. When the current generation of pastors retires, there are simply not enough mature believers there to replace them. It is essential that solid theological and pastoral training schemes are made not only available but accessible, and are enthusiastically encouraged. The church in Japan must rise to the task of telling the next generation the praiseworthy deeds of the Lord, that they might not forget His deeds but keep His commands (v. 7). We too must take note of the need to raise up future leaders for our own nations and for the global church.

PRAYER

Heavenly Father, I pray for each of Your beloved children in Japan. Please help them to grow closer to Christ day by day, looking more and more like Him. Help them to live radical lives for You, cutting across the grain of their culture for Your glory. Please strengthen the churches and raise up leaders among the next generation who will boldly proclaim Your Word and faithfully serve the body of Christ. I pray that the church in Japan would grow in number, in depth and in love for You.

DAY 25

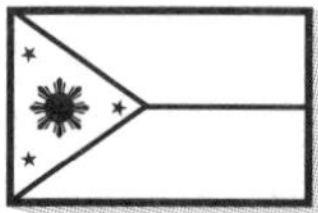

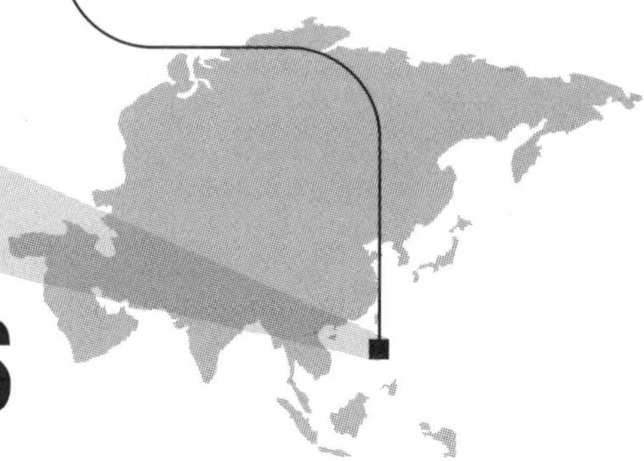

PHILIPPINES

Part 1

You arrive in Manila, the capital city of the Philippines, with a strange feeling of familiarity. For once, you are not overwhelmed by the sights, sounds and smells of a new location, nor do you feel that hard-to-define sense of being out of your comfort zone. Manila is worlds apart from other Southeast Asian capitals you have visited. Rather than being exotically Asian, much about the city is reminiscent of the West. It isn't until you step into some local museums that you discover why. In the early 1900s, American influence was strong here.

The Philippine archipelago had been under colonial rule since the mid-1500s; Spain was the first to lay claim to the islands, before ceding to the US in the late 19th century. There was even a brief period of Japanese occupation during the Second World War. As the Philippines slowly fought for independence, the US helped and hindered in many ways before recognising the land as a stand-alone nation in 1946. But the American influence can be seen clearly even today with the nation's rectangular-shaped network of broad streets and open avenues.

Basketball is a hugely popular sport here, one of the few nations to favour it so heavily. The political system is also familiar, with a president, Senate and House of Representatives. Thankfully, the Philippines also maintains true freedom of belief unlike most Asian nations. The country is considered to be overwhelmingly Christian, but the vast majority follow Catholic traditions. It saddens you to think that so many here may have grown up identifying as Christians and yet failing to understand the gospel of God's grace in Christ.

BIBLE VERSE

'Not everyone who says to me, "Lord, Lord," will enter the kingdom of heaven, but only the one who does the will of my Father who is in heaven'
(Mt. 7:21).

REFLECTION

It is remarkable how pervasive Catholicism is in the Philippines. Churches are found everywhere, and most hospitals and schools are named after a saint. As it is rare for Christianity to be welcomed in this part of the world, there is reason to feel encouraged. However, when it comes to salvation, it is not enough to be 'a good Catholic' or to attend mass regularly. Salvation comes through faith alone, by grace alone, in Christ alone. Many here have never heard the gospel explained, despite considering themselves Christians. Jesus warns that there will be those who recognise Him as Lord yet will not enter the kingdom of heaven. It is a humbling warning. Do you belong wholly and truly to Christ? The Catholic majority in the Philippines must heed this warning too, and ensure they live in the light of the one, true and glorious gospel of Jesus Christ.

PRAYER

Lord, I thank You that there is freedom in the Philippines and that the glory of Your name can be declared freely and widely. Please use those who trust in the cross and resurrection of Jesus to witness to others, imploring their neighbours to consider Jesus' warning in Matthew 7. Lord, please grow the evangelical church here and help them take advantage of every opportunity to proclaim the truth about Your grace. May many who call themselves Christians truly be welcomed into Your kingdom, for Your glory.

DAY 26

PHILIPPINES

Part 2

The religious freedom found here in the Philippines stands out against the hostile attitude of the nation's neighbours. Indonesia, Brunei and Malaysia are predominantly Muslim nations, each with varying degrees of restrictive legislation in place against other faiths or against conversions away from Islam.

As Diwa serves you a cool drink in a local cafe, she explains that the Philippines have been targeted by Islamic extremist groups in the past. In 2017, a faction allegiant to ISIS, known as the Maute group, laid claim to the city of Marawi. Philippine forces attempted to capture the group's leaders, only to find that the city was full of armed Maute fighters. Foreign militants had joined the group from Indonesia, Malaysia, Saudi Arabia and other nations. For five months, conflict raged, with civilians used as human shields and child warriors recruited from as young as ten years of age. With the area placed on lockdown and fighters setting homes ablaze, a mass evacuation ensued. Families abandoned their homes and possessions, fleeing in their thousands in search of safety. Over 90% of the population left their homes.

During this period, opportunities arose for local Christian groups to meet the needs of people who had moved out of Marawi. Through the provision of vital aid such as food, clean water and accommodation, these groups established firm relationships with many families. As the conflict raged on, they shared the gospel with people who had not given their lives to Christ.

When Philippine forces took back the city about six months later, the process of cleaning up and restoring the city of Marawi began. Peace had come, but Diwa admits she fears that there remains potential for further conflict in the future.

BIBLE VERSE

'This is what the Lord Almighty said: "Administer true justice; show mercy and compassion to one another. Do not oppress the widow or the fatherless, the foreigner or the poor. Do not plot evil against each other"'
(Zech. 7:9–10).

REFLECTION

The fallout from the conflict in Marawi continues, and the restoration effort will take many years. Numerous buildings are yet to be repaired or rebuilt, and thousands of families are still unable to return to their home city. While it is impossible for us to imagine such a sudden city-wide conflict, our hearts go out to families affected by such incidents the world over. Zechariah reminds us of the Lord's heart for all people on earth, and so we praise God for those believers reaching the afflicted and bringing Christ to them, showing mercy and compassion just as Christ did on the cross. Sadly, many in the Philippines and across the world continue to plot evil against one other. We must vigilantly guard our own hearts, seeking to lift others up rather than do them harm with our words and actions.

PRAYER

Lord, I pray for families who have been afflicted by conflict in the Philippines. I ask that You would draw close to them as they live with such traumatic events in their past. Lord, please undo the plans and plots of those who seek to do evil. Thank You for faithful servants displaying Your compassion and mercy to those in need around the world today. I pray that their witness will serve to glorify You and bring many to saving faith.

DAY 27

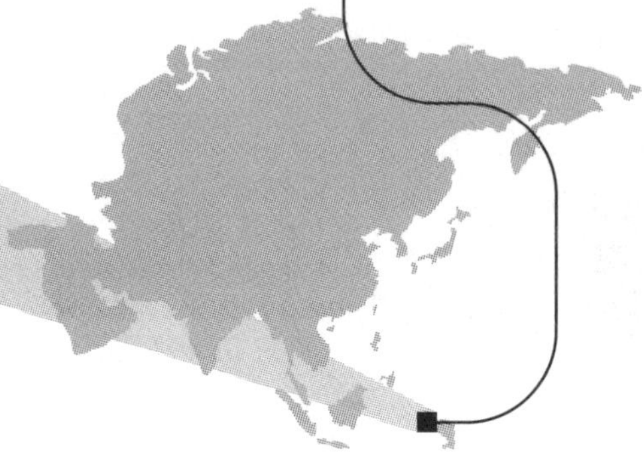

INDONESIA

Part 1

Indonesia consists of over 17,000 islands, of which around 6000 are inhabited. It is the world's most populous Muslim-majority country, incorporating both traditional and modern approaches to Islam. As you fly into Jakarta, on the island of Java, you arrive at a place like no other. With numerous cities scattered between the 38 mountains which form a spine from east to west, this is the most populous island in the world. It is clear that you will not see everything in your few days here!

Jakarta, the national capital, lies towards the west of the island. Here, the climate is wet and humid, allowing lush green vegetation to form the city's backdrop. In contrast, the downtown streets are a dirty, noisy hive of activity, ranking among the world's most congested locations. Multi-lane highways are regularly saturated with cars, taxis and trucks jostling for position in queues which stretch for miles.

At the heart of the city, colonial architecture is dwarfed by modern skyscrapers housing hotels, shops, offices and private apartments. However, as you explore further, you find crumbling roads leading to suburban areas and, often, to slums tucked away between rivers, railway lines and construction sites. Here, ramshackle huts of wood and corrugated iron line informal pathways clogged with litter. Young children roam in groups, their filthy clothes long outworn. They are unsupervised – their parents and older siblings occupied with whatever work they can find to feed the family that evening. They have few possessions and regular flooding has destroyed what belongings they once treasured. As you look along the chaotic row of haphazard homes, your heart breaks in the knowledge that these people have no sure foundation for their homes, their incomes or their eternal futures.

BIBLE VERSE

'Therefore everyone who hears these words of mine and puts them into practice is like a wise man who built his house on the rock' (Mt. 7:24).

REFLECTION

In the West, strict codes ensure that buildings are structurally sound and set on stable ground. However, the same is not true for the poor in Asia, many of whom have to build their own homes in whatever space they can find, using whatever materials are available. In Jakarta, makeshift homes stand on stilts above water and lie within inches of passing trains. When strong winds come or water levels rise, the family home is endangered, just like those who built their house on the sand in Jesus' parable (v. 26). But how much more is our eternal future in danger when we do not build our lives on the words of Christ – the only sure foundation! The people of Jakarta build their lives on the unstable ground of Islam, constantly unsure whether they will be accepted by God and simply hoping for mercy. If only they would look to the cross.

PRAYER

Heavenly Father, thank You for the love that You have shown me. Thank You that at the cross of Jesus You poured out grace and mercy in abundance, and that in His words I can find a sure foundation. My house will not fall! I pray that You might work through Christians in Jakarta to share the good news of Christ so that many would find salvation. Lord, I pray particularly that the poor would find hope in the midst of their daily struggles.

DAY 28

INDONESIA

Part 2

Having seen some of the hardest sights this city has to offer, today you take in more of the culture. Inside the national museum, you discover stone images of tribal kings from over 1000 years ago, alongside golden treasures and beautiful fabrics. You spend some time admiring the national monument outside about Indonesia's struggle for independence, before heading across the park to the Grand Istiqlal (Liberty) Mosque. With an impressive dome stretching 45 metres in diameter, this is the largest mosque in Southeast Asia. Although simple in design, it represents a powerful statement of this officially secular nation's alignment with Islam.

To learn more, you meet Mochtar over lunch in the Mangga Besar district, where he guarantees a good meal. Having struggled to decide between beef rendang, soto ayam and the more familiar satay, you finally order nasi goreng and are delighted when a huge portion of fried rice appears! As you tuck into the food, Mochtar tells you about his job teaching the 'holy books' in a Muslim theological school. He explains that since the struggle for independence began, the national identity has been increasingly rooted in Islam, drawing a dividing line between Indonesia and its European colonisers. He suggests that this is one of many reasons why Indonesian Muslims neglect to read any book other than the Quran and the Hadith, despite the Law, the psalms and the gospels being held up as 'holy books' in Islamic texts. As a believer, Mochtar has a remarkable opportunity to teach the good news of Christ – as foreshadowed in the Old Testament – to some of the brightest and most devout Muslims in the city. Of course, he must do so with care and wisdom, but he thanks God for the opportunity he has been given.

BIBLE VERSE

'So if the Son sets you free, you will be free indeed' (John 8:36).

REFLECTION

The history of colonialism in Asia, Africa and elsewhere is founded upon greed, exploitation and oppression. While many highlight the positive influences of colonisation, it is not hard to understand why nations like Indonesia fought for their independence. The national monument and Istiqlal Mosque are two lasting celebrations of that achievement. But according to Jesus, these people have not yet found freedom. Only when they come to the Son will they be truly free. This truth was hard for Jesus' Jewish audience to take. They were Abraham's descendants (v. 33) and saw no need to be liberated. But Jesus explained that they were slaves to sin. The same is true of the majority in 'liberated' Indonesia, and the same was once true of you and me. Those who have no room for Jesus' Word are living enslaved by sin and in desperate need of liberation.

PRAYER

Lord God, thank You so much for the freedom that I have found in You. Thank You that You gave Your Word and helped my heart to receive it. Lord, I pray for those countries which suffered under colonial rule. Please lift them out of difficult situations. And Lord, I pray that You would help the people of Indonesia to see that they are not truly free. Please enable Your Word to spread among the unreached in that nation, so that many might hear of Your Son and find true freedom in Him.

DAY 29

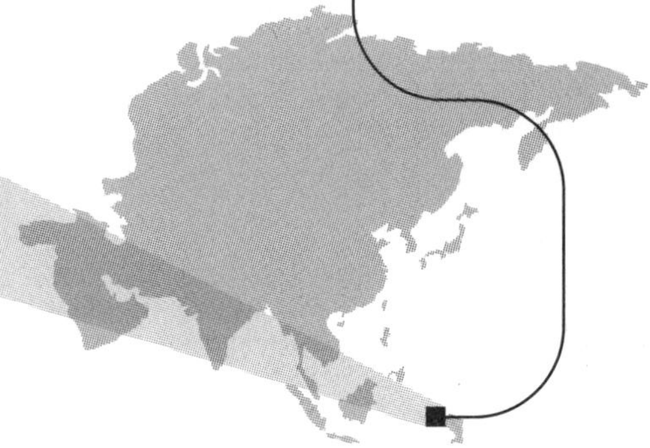

INDONESIA

Part 3

You travel by boat to a small island. It is a rough and choppy ride, which leaves you feeling queasy. A lady named Novita meets you and, as you travel towards the town, explains the island's recent history. It is only a few years since fighting broke out, with Muslim groups partially succeeding in driving out the Christians. Both lives and homes were lost in the conflict.

Novita introduces you to Pastor Andika, who leads a church in his village. Although he is fluent in Indonesian, he and his community connect most strongly with the local language. Only a few thousand people share this mother tongue. They make up just one of the hundreds of people groups in Indonesia who do not have access to Scripture in their heart language, including many groups who have been reached with the gospel. The result is that although the good news has been shared with whole communities and professions of the Christian faith have been made, deep, heart-level understanding of the gospel remains rare. Elements of legalism and superstition take root in the absence of the Scriptures.

Pastor Andika explains that he has been blessed with good teaching and the ability to understand Indonesian translations of Scripture, but many pastors and congregations are not so fortunate. So one of the deepest needs among Indonesia's Christian communities is to have the Bible in their own languages, so that pastors might benefit from a sound understanding of God's Word and churches might be built upon a firm foundation. For now, Andika prays that the Spirit would continue to guide and lead the nation's many untrained pastors.

BIBLE VERSE

'You will keep in perfect peace those whose minds are steadfast, because they trust in you'
(Is. 26:3).

REFLECTION

Being driven away from your town or village because of your faith is not something many of us will ever have contemplated. Nor is the idea of having zero access to God's Word to lead, guide, encourage and inspire us, let alone for those who lead our churches. Much work remains to be done in translating and distributing Bibles in each of Indonesia's many languages. How wonderful it would be for all who profess Christian faith, and many who currently do not, to truly know the grace and mercy of God displayed in Christ. How glorious it would be for every Indonesian believer to be able to study the Scriptures day by day, learning together, growing in love for the Lord and becoming increasingly steadfast as He keeps them in perfect peace.

PRAYER

Heavenly Father, thank You for the church in Indonesia. Thank You for the millions of people who know and love You, and for their witness in a hostile environment. I pray that You would sustain those who have no Bible in their language. I pray that You would give profound wisdom and guidance to those leading churches in such circumstances. Lord, please provide the necessary workers to produce Bibles in these many languages and make Your church here a shining light in the midst of a Muslim majority.

DAY 30

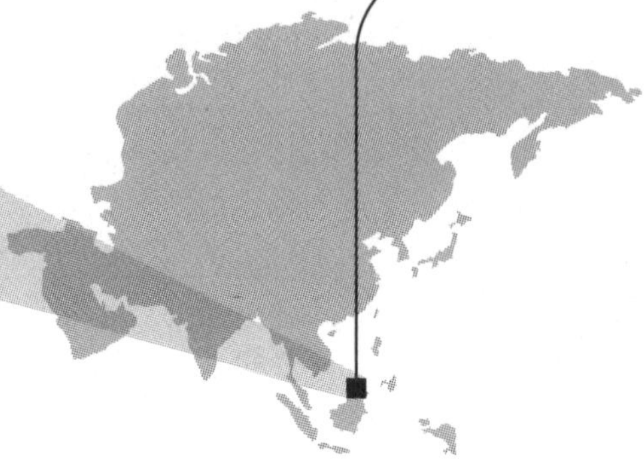

BRUNEI

Part 1

On your journey to Brunei's small and peaceful capital city, Bandar Seri Begawan, signs remind you that carrying drugs into the country could incur the death penalty. Under Sharia law, several other offences could, theoretically, result in the same fate. Brunei made headlines in 2019 after announcing that adultery or homosexual relations would be added to that list, although the sultan backtracked after international outcry. Nevertheless, these laws highlight the Muslim bedrock on which this Malay-majority society is built.

This tiny nation lies on the northern coast of Borneo, surrounded by the Malaysian state of Sarawak. On the surface, it appears to be a prosperous nation of peaceful, contented Muslims. Families own large houses and have more cars per household than anywhere else on earth. But dig a little deeper and a different picture emerges. After walking through the quiet streets, you head to a restaurant. Some young adults at the next table share jovial conversation but, as their generation is not receiving the benefits bestowed upon their parents, discontent is setting in. They work in shops and offices, yet consider themselves unemployed until they are offered the government job which would set them up for life.

State-controlled television broadcasts daily prayers from the corner of the restaurant. The majority here are devout Muslims, but young adults like these find themselves increasingly unsure of their faith. They daren't express this, not even to one another. The close-knit population of under half a million and the presence of secret police on every street mean news travels fast, making the expression of one's political or religious feelings somewhat dangerous. The consequences of apostasy are severe, making it painfully costly to leave Islam behind. Alas, the rituals and routine go on.

BIBLE VERSE

'Do not be afraid of those who kill the body but cannot kill the soul' (Mt. 10:28).

REFLECTION

How might Jesus respond to those young adults afraid to renounce their Islamic heritage? Having sent His disciples out as sheep among wolves, Jesus urged them to fear not man but God. God has not only the power to judge (v. 28), but also knows and cares for them: 'you are worth more than many sparrows' (v. 31). Elsewhere, Jesus said, 'Look at the birds of the air; they do not sow or reap or stow away in barns, and yet your heavenly Father feeds them. Are you not much more valuable than they?' (Mt. 6:26). Perhaps Jesus' words to those young adults would be similar: 'Do not be afraid of men judging you for abandoning Islam. Instead, fear the One who numbers the hairs on your head and will welcome you home with outstretched arms.' How precious it would be to see Bruneian Malays turning to the Lord!

PRAYER

Heavenly Father, I pray for those people in Brunei who are caught up in the traditions and rituals of a religion they have lost faith in. Help them to seek truth and give them opportunities to hear the good news of Your Son, Jesus. I pray that You would help many to discover the gospel and have the boldness to count the cost and begin following Jesus. Help me to stand for Christ too, being unashamed of my Saviour and bringing glory to Your name.

DAY 31

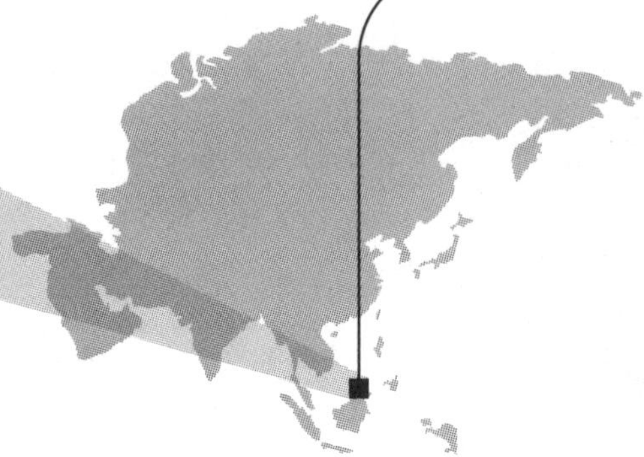

BRUNEI

Part 2

You will not read about it in the local newspaper, but sections of the government are becoming restless. The gradual exhaustion of the country's oil supply is raising difficult questions about the future. Leaders are desperate to ensure peace and prosperity, but are unable to offer the next generation the privileges enjoyed by their parents and grandparents.

Tourism is increasingly being viewed as a vital industry, but as you walk along the riverbank on a pleasant, sunny afternoon, you find the cafes closed at times when a tourist hotspot should be brimming with activity. One local suggests that you walk through the famous water village with its raised boardwalks above the river, and points you towards the tourist information office. However, you find that they have no maps of the city and few activities to recommend. This nation will have to adapt to survive, but to whom will they turn? Nobody has the experience necessary to successfully induce a culture shift or to ignite a tourist industry from nothing. For many, the only answer will be to rely on Allah's will, but this will be no source of peace until a solution is found.

Of course, the Muslim Malays, whom this nation is designed to serve, are well aware of the existence of other religions. A small number of churches and temples exist, but these only accommodate those who migrate here for work and are kept at arm's length through laws prohibiting the promotion of other faiths. Malays here know little about the Christianity, Buddhism and Hinduism practised by other communities, and the government is eager to ensure that citizens are never persuaded to count the cost, take up their cross and follow Christ.

BIBLE VERSE

'Whoever loves money never has enough; whoever loves wealth is never satisfied with their income. This too is meaningless' (Ecc. 5:10).

REFLECTION

Governments and leaders are often focused on boosting the national economy. Of course, this can bring about much good in terms of reducing poverty and protecting the vulnerable. But if increased wealth is our goal, we will never have enough. This is true at a national and an individual level. Perhaps you have felt that tension yourself. We can go chasing after material comfort, but we will never feel satisfied or secure in the fleeting comforts of wealth. It is meaningless. Many people in Brunei are wealthy yet discontent, comfortable yet afraid, devout yet lost. They submit out of fear to worldly desires and false gods when their greatest need is not for earthly security but eternal life. This nation needs the hope and peace found only by acknowledging and delighting in the authority of Christ.

PRAYER

Lord, I pray that You would help believers in Brunei to live peaceably in that society and shine like lights on a hill. Please make the churches there a powerful witness to Your glorious grace. And I pray that as people in Brunei look for comfort and security in worldly riches and false gods, they would discover the certain hope of salvation found in Christ. Lord, please make the gospel more accessible in the nation and help many to find true satisfaction in You.

DAY 32

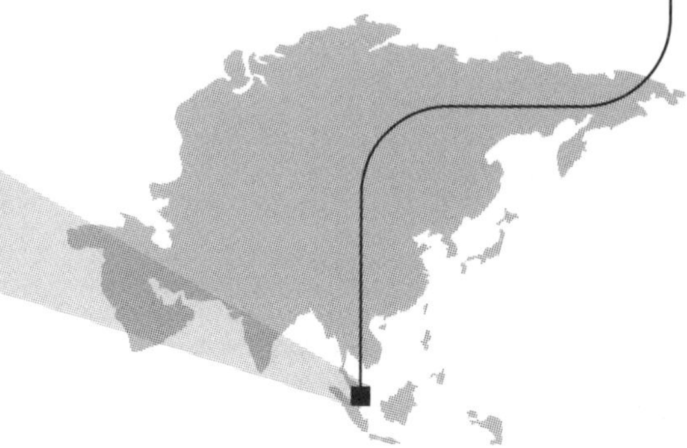

MALAYSIA

Part 1

You are making your way through the throbbing streets of Kuala Lumpur, the capital of Malaysia. There are people everywhere! Many streets, while not officially pedestrianised, have been colonised by chairs and tables as restaurants and cafes extend into the road. Those dining here enjoy all kinds of East and Southeast Asian food as they soak up the electric atmosphere. Illuminated by faintly buzzing neon lights, conversation and laughter flow freely. Families embrace before taking their seats and groups of women set down their many bags of shopping to eat. Meanwhile, tables full of tourists look on curiously at the community and camaraderie which surround them.

Towering over the scene are numerous high-rise buildings, home to apartments and offices. Their sleek modern appearance is a stark contrast to the rough-and-ready streets below. You also notice the sheer diversity around you. Aside from the predominant native Malay people, there are many Indians and Chinese. You hear conversations in an array of languages, recognising a little Mandarin and Hindi being spoken, alongside several languages and dialects you could not begin to place.

Kuala Lumpur, like Malaysia in general, is full of not only life but all kinds of people. As you explore the city, you come across a wide variety of religious places of worship: mosques, Buddhist and Hindu temples, and Christian churches. With such a plethora of beliefs and ideologies co-existing, it can be hard to convince people of the unique offer of the gospel and the cross as the only way to find salvation. This begs the important question: how will these people come to know Christ?

BIBLE VERSE

'Salvation is found in no one else, for there is no other name under heaven given to mankind by which we must be saved' (Acts 4:12).

REFLECTION

The melting pot of Malaysia is home to communities from numerous faith backgrounds. Each has a different set of beliefs regarding the way they should live and what happens in the next life, if they believe in an afterlife at all. Some believe their way is the right way; others believe that all religions are simply different paths to the same God. In a place where so many faiths are practised openly, Acts 4:12 is an essential reminder that there is only one way in which salvation can be found – through faith in Jesus Christ. How important it is, then, for the gospel to be made known in places like Malaysia, so that all might hear of the saving power found in Jesus.

PRAYER

Lord, thank You that Jesus is the way, the truth and the life. I thank You for opening my eyes to this truth but I pray for the billions in this world who believe that there is some other way to You. Lord, have mercy on them as they seek to find salvation through works, through false gods and even from within themselves. I pray in particular for the people of Malaysia. Please help many to hear of Your Son and trust Him as their Lord and personal Saviour.

DAY 33

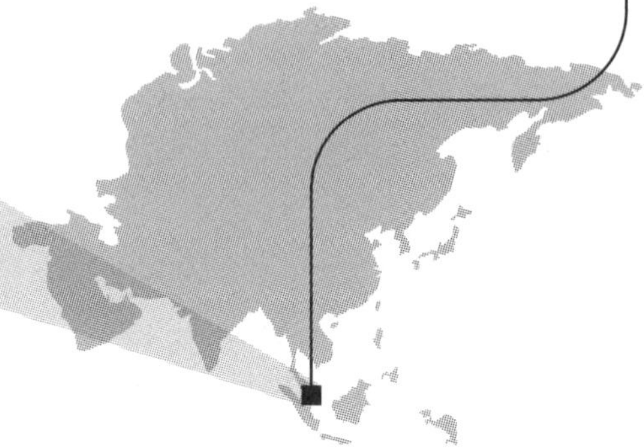

MALAYSIA

Part 2

Malaysia's contradictions surrounding freedom of belief become increasingly clear as you spend time here. You have previously noted the vast diversity of people, languages, nationalities and religious sites, but upon visiting a local church, you find no indigenous Malay people in attendance. While being officially secular and enshrining freedom of belief in law, Malaysia legislates strictly against abandoning Islam. In the national constitution, ethnic Malays are automatically defined as Muslim. In nearly every state, it is illegal for Malays to be anything but Muslim. Those who do convert suffer persecution in various forms. Malaysia has policies in place which favour Muslim Malays, helping them secure housing, good schooling and reduced taxes. Anyone converting to another faith loses all these privileges and may even be detained.

Speaking to some of those at the church you are visiting, you discover that Christian materials in the Malay language are restricted by the government. It also keeps a close eye on the activities of the church and strictly forbids evangelism to Malay people. Outreach does take place, however, and many have come to faith through encounters with those from other ethnic groups. There is much prayer for the Malay and a deep desire to reach them more effectively, but the church is in a precarious position. For now, secret evangelism must suffice.

It is a bittersweet feeling to worship in this church full of believers from such diverse backgrounds. The Lord is bringing many to Himself through this church's ministry, yet how wonderful it would be for many Malays to be worshipping alongside you as a part of this church family. You pray with the believers here that God might allow it to happen soon.

BIBLE VERSE

'Live as free people, but do not use your freedom as a cover-up for evil; live as God's slaves' (1 Pet. 2:16).

REFLECTION

A strange, false freedom exists here. On the one hand, freedom of belief results in the presence of people from many different nationalities and faiths. On the other, severe restrictions are placed upon the Malay people. Even if they heard the gospel and wished to put their faith in Christ, the law demands that they remain Muslim. Many who read 1 Peter 2:16 might think it a kind of false freedom as well. How can we live as free people yet also as God's slaves? But, unlike in Malaysia, there is no contradiction here. In Christ, we have the privilege of living free from sin and for our Creator. Only when we live in a manner pleasing to God can we enjoy life to the full. True freedom is found in surrendering our lives to the Lordship of our good and just God.

PRAYER

Lord, thank You for setting me free from sin through Your Son. Thank You that I can enjoy true freedom when I live totally for You. I pray for those in Malaysia who live a life of false freedom. Please change hearts and move the government to allow Malay people to become Christians without legal impediment. I pray that churches would stand ready to reach and welcome these people in Your name, and that they might find true freedom in living for You.

DAY 34

MALAYSIA

Part 3

You leave the metropolis of Kuala Lumpur behind, travelling east to the Sarawak region on the island of Borneo. On the flight, you observe the thick jungle which cloaks the island. As memories of nature documentaries are stirred, you wonder how many orangutans live beneath the lush green canopy below! Borneo is the largest island in Asia and uniquely governed by three different nations. Much of the south is governed by Indonesia, while the entire nation of Brunei is found along the northern coast and the rest belongs to Malaysia. Nevertheless, this feels like a very different country. Gone are the towering skyscrapers and cityscapes of the capital city. Sibu, the city in which you land, is significantly less developed. As you head out towards the jungle, the settlements become increasingly basic.

The region's majority group are the Dayak people. They live along the banks of major rivers, inhabiting distinctive long houses, each of which accommodates around 30 people. As recently as the 1800s, it was common practice for them to collect the severed heads of tribal enemies to present to their leaders. Skulls would then be put on display, serving as an indication of status and power. This practice was outlawed and has mostly faded away, although unconfirmed reports suggest headhunting still occurs today.

As you walk among the wooden Dayak settlements bedded into the jungle around them, you are encouraged to hear from your guide, Umar, of great gospel growth over the past century. He informs you that around 15% of this small people group now confess the name of Christ! Yet there are many more on this island who have never heard of Jesus at all. Secluded in the depths of the jungles of Borneo are countless communities whose lives remain untouched by the gospel.

BIBLE VERSE

'After this I looked, and there before me was a great multitude that no one could count, from every nation, tribe, people and language, standing before the throne and before the Lamb' (Rev. 7:9).

REFLECTION

The history of the Dayak people is an encouraging one. Although their recent history contains much violence, horrific practices such as headhunting are largely resigned to the past. The gospel may have played a part in this, but the Dayak serve as a reminder of the great challenge of reaching remote tribal groups. Many unreached tribes live incredibly differently to the urban population, and the work of deciphering languages and understanding cultures will take many, many years.
So the apostle John's vision is encouraging! Among the uncountable multitudes gathered around the throne of God are people from every tribe. Those who are yet to receive the gospel in our day will one day hear, and we will spend an eternity with those believers. Lord, hasten the day when Your Word reaches these people!

PRAYER

Lord, thank You for Your faithfulness over many years in allowing the good news to reach the Dayak people. I praise You that I will enjoy the blessing of sharing eternity with them. I pray for those involved in tribal outreach, particularly in this region of Malaysia. Please raise up faithful witnesses who are prepared to learn languages and cross cultures. May many tribal groups untouched by Your gospel come to hear it soon and place their trust in You!

DAY 35

THAILAND

Part 1

As you arrive by plane at Bangkok, you could be in one of a number of major cities, but the city itself takes on a life and character of its own. Narrow backstreets play host to restaurants serving food from around the world, while shopping malls offer well-known brands next to an abundance of mini-market stalls. Skyscrapers climb towards the bright blue sky, appearing almost at random from behind the more traditional three- and four-storey buildings which line the busy streets. The rush of traffic is constant, with the noise of engines broken only by the occasional rattle of sky trains passing by overhead.

On a tour of the city, you encounter countless historic buildings and ornate Buddhist temples – not to mention the bustling alleys and markets which are an experience in and of themselves! As night falls, stall owners begin to pack up their wares while other areas spring to life. Garish neon lights set the tone in the city's three red-light districts and the streets become increasingly crowded as revellers arrive to party the night away in nightclubs and go-go bars.

Eight million people live here and conduct their daily business to this boisterous backdrop. They work in the offices, shops, taxis and bars, worship in the temples, mosques and churches, and relax in the parks and cinemas. But for the city's endless stream of visitors, Bangkok is a potent distraction from the norm. Whether you are visiting to work, dance, drink or pay for sex, there is a constant temptation to put the rest of the world behind and simply live in the moment.

BIBLE VERSE

'... those who live like this will not inherit the kingdom of God' (Gal. 5:21).

REFLECTION

The world is full of temptations to indulge the 'flesh'. Adverts compel us to find fulfilment in fashion, technology and holidays, while influencers urge us to be 'true to ourselves' and live for 'number one'. While these temptations seem more prevalent in places like Bangkok, they are simply exaggerated. Galatians 5 lists numerous acts of the flesh, ranging from sexual immorality and drunkenness to hatred and selfish ambition. In contrast, the fruit of the Spirit is love, joy, peace, forbearance, kindness, goodness, faithfulness, gentleness and self-control – characteristics all believers are called to display, not just those who aspire to be pastors or missionaries! How will people in Bangkok hear the gospel? Through Christians who live there being distinctive in their behaviour, loving in their engagement with others, and bold in speaking of Christ.

PRAYER

Lord, forgive me when I succumb to worldly temptations, and help me not to judge others when I too am fully dependent on Your grace. Please reach into the lives of those living in Bangkok. Help Christians to be bold in sharing the gospel and godly in their conduct, so that many might hear the good news of Jesus and see it lived out in a glorious and compelling way. Help those visiting Bangkok for escapism to realise that true freedom is found not in alcohol, parties or sex, but through forgiveness and acceptance in Christ.

DAY 36

THAILAND

Part 2

You hail a taxi and travel along busy roads to a trendy bakery in the Bang Na district. In its pleasantly cool interior is an enticing bakery counter to your right, with a range of stylish, handcrafted jewellery displayed opposite.

Kamlai is its manager. She welcomes you with a warm smile and explains the work going on here over fresh coffee. She shares her passion for reaching bar girls with the gospel, before taking you upstairs to see where some of those who have escaped the sex industry now produce jewellery. Others work in the bakery downstairs, with some even sent to receive high-quality education. The stairway is lined by images of smiling girls, each with their own powerful story of a life transformed by this centre and by Christ.

'This is Noi,' Kamlai says, pointing at one joyful face. 'Her parents died and she worked in bars to pay her siblings' school fees, performing all the extras people expect. She struggled with drugs and even went to jail while her two daughters disappeared with their respective fathers. Her aunt was planning to sell her to a massage parlour in South Korea. Thank God we could offer her a way out! She really struggled to adapt to a new life, but God changed her heart. She grew in Christ and married a Christian man. They have a daughter and share the gospel together in her home region.'

The people of Noi's home region are considered unreached by the gospel. There are very few believers and no established churches. Through every dark and painful situation in her life, God has been preparing Noi to tell her people of His glorious grace for the very first time.

BIBLE VERSE

'She is clothed with strength and dignity; she can laugh at the days to come'
(Prov. 31:25).

REFLECTION

Thousands of Asian women live at the mercy of those who exploit their poverty for personal financial gain. Some women reluctantly join the sex industry to support their families, while others are lured in through false promises of safe work. Their exploiters control them, often through drug addiction, stripping away any sense of self-worth. However, each of these women is fearfully and wonderfully made in God's image – not worthless or far from the Lord. In fact, many are desperately seeking the sense of value and dignity found only in relationship with our loving Father. Proverbs 31 depicts a wife of noble character who provides for her family (v. 15), works hard (v. 17), speaks with wisdom (v. 26) and fears the Lord (v. 30). Through Kamlai's work, God graciously transformed Noi's life, lifting her up to be a wife of noble character and His ambassador to an unreached people.

PRAYER

Thank You, Lord, for welcoming those who are weary and burdened, downcast and broken-hearted. Thank You for opposing the proud and showing favour to the humble. I praise You for the wonderful grace You worked in Noi's life, and in the lives of many others who have escaped the sex industry. Thank You that they have found freedom in Christ and discovered new purpose in Him. Help them to be women of noble character who live for You, making the most of all You give them and glorifying Your name wherever You may lead them.

DAY 37

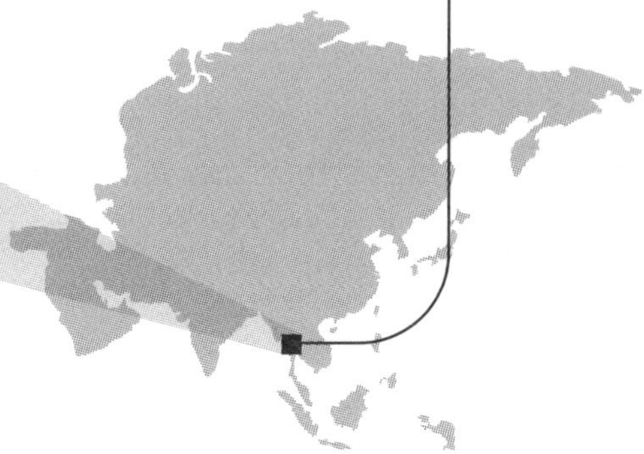

THAILAND

Part 3

There is more to Thailand than the bright lights of Bangkok, so let's head south! A short flight over rocky mountains and the dark green canopy of impenetrable tropical forest takes you to the former Pattani kingdom. The provinces of Pattani, Yala and Narathiwat have been recognised as Thai territory for centuries, much to the dismay of the Malay population. Continued uprisings necessitate a heavy police and military presence, though the occasional violence rarely endangers civilian life. Most protest more peacefully, shunning Thai language and beliefs in favour of their Malay and Islamic heritage.

The colourful buildings of the quiet city rest beneath a warm sun, as Thai flags and images of the royal family remind locals who is in charge. The government did fund the construction of a large new mosque as a gesture of goodwill, but many refuse to worship there.

You enter a tea shop to the sound of caged birds, a common feature in this region where birdsong competitions attract hundreds of entrants. You meet Somchai who is ethnically Thai. He has moved south to reach the Malay people and explains the challenges of this work. Even getting started was tricky, with churches in Thailand reluctant to support Muslim outreach when ministry 'success' is clearer among the peoples in the northern hills. Somchai describes his struggles learning the Pattani Malay language and meeting people in close-knit and closed-off communities. Nevertheless, he and others are making inroads by offering English teaching, sports coaching and other services to local groups. Somchai knows that success will require strong relationships and is asking the Lord to help him be salt and light: to live a godly life and take gospel opportunities among a community who know nothing of Christ.

BIBLE VERSE

'I have become all things to all people so that by all possible means I might save some' (1 Cor. 9:22).

REFLECTION

Have you ever been in a situation where nobody knows your language? Perhaps you were trying to purchase food on holiday or get directions to a tourist attraction? A few hand gestures later you were probably sorted! For workers like Somchai, learning a language is not enough. Paul sought to become like a Jew to win the Jews, like one under the law to win those under the law, and like the weak to win the weak (vv. 20–22). Working across cultures requires adaptation and hard work, so cross-cultural workers must be in it for the long haul. It can be years before they see real signs of fruit. There are no shortcuts. Instead, we must trust that God will bless the efforts of His faithful servants. Whether we send or support missionaries or go ourselves, it is vital that we back them for the long haul.

PRAYER

Heavenly Father, thank You for Somchai and others around the world who are willing to uproot themselves, learn a new language and adapt to a new culture. Please give them an abundance of wisdom! Sustain them when opportunities for fellowship are scarce and bless their labours with a harvest of many souls saved for eternity. Help those of us back home to be faithful in prayer and dedicated in our support for these workers, especially through those hard times when we cannot see Your hand at work.

DAY 38

THAILAND

Part 4

With one day left in Thailand, it's time to head north to Chiang Mai. This city is a real hotspot for tourism, with countless markets and temples surrounded by beautiful countryside. Missionaries have been in Thailand for around 250 years. However, less than 1% of the nation's population are Christians and around three quarters of believers are found in the hills north of the city. There are few ethnic Thai Christians.

You venture out to meet some believers from the Lahu people group, but are surprised by what you find: this free nation is one of the wealthiest in Southeast Asia, yet these people cannot access a Bible which they understand. A number of translations have been produced over the years, but these have always been in high language solely understood by the elite. People save up to buy one of these expensive Bibles, only to read one page and find it incomprehensible.

However, you are told that a delivery of easy-to-read versions is arriving today! People gather, young and old alike, excited to receive God's Word in a language they understand. A truck pulls up, boxes are unloaded and a ceremony of thanksgiving takes place before the Bibles are handed out, one per family. Until now, these people have relied entirely on the pastor for their spiritual understanding. Now they will be able to read God's Word for themselves! A group of young Lahu adults are sat to your left. They have never understood the gospel before, but today they will go home and read God's Word for themselves for the first time. In the coming weeks, they will each accept Jesus as their personal Saviour, and you will later hear that they have all gone on to work as evangelists in the local area!

BIBLE VERSE

'How sweet are your words to my taste,
sweeter than honey to my mouth!'
(Ps. 119:103).

REFLECTION

The story of the young adults is true. After reading the Bible in words they could understand, they were saved and chose to live wholeheartedly for the Lord. And yet so many groups in the northern hills and among the ethnic Thai people cannot access God's Word. This presents a twofold challenge. First, can we say with the psalmist that God's Word is sweeter than honey (v. 103), that we love His law (v. 97) and that His commands are always with us (v. 98)? Second, do we see the urgent need to provide Bibles in languages people can understand, so that they might find God's Word to be a lamp for their feet and a light for their path (v. 105)? May more and more people in Asia come to know the Lord and praise His name!

PRAYER

Lord, I thank You for those in the hills and among the ethnic Thai people who have come to trust in You. I thank You for your Word, which is sweeter than honey; help me to delight in it each day. I pray that more and more people might have access to it! Please help those translating Scripture to do so faithfully and clearly. Help those distributing Bibles to get them to the right people, even when worldly authorities seek to stop them. Lord, please change many lives and communities as Your Word is received, read and believed.

DAY 39

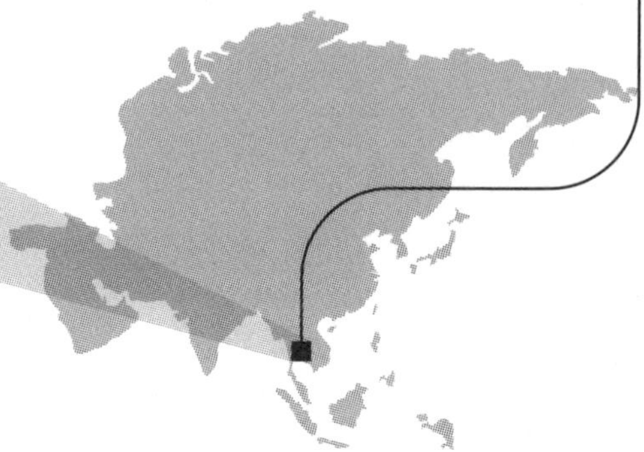

CAMBODIA

Part 1

The bustling streets of Cambodia's capital, Phnom Penh, are full of markets, traders and tourists. A hotspot for travellers, entire streets are set aside to accommodate the millions who visit each year. Everywhere you turn, you see westerners with big rucksacks wearing garish clothing clearly bought on their travels.

To understand Cambodia, you need look no further than its two most popular tourist destinations. Angkor Wat is a temple so identified with Cambodia that it features on the national flag. One of the world's seven modern wonders, this is the largest religious monument on earth. The temple has served both the Buddhist and Hindu faiths during its 900-year history, reflecting the nation's tumultuous history – the dominant faith changed as ruling powers came and went. Today, Buddhism is the predominant faith, with millions attempting to perform good works in the hope of a favourable reincarnation. And then there are the infamous Killing Fields – areas full of mass graves. In the late 70s, under the leadership of dictator Pol Pot, the communist Khmer Rouge regime arrested and executed anyone with connections – suspected or proven – to former or foreign governments. Many were subjected to this attempted genocide, from foreign ethnicities to Cambodian religious groups such as Buddhist monks and Christians. While figures vary, it is estimated that between two and three million people were killed.

Cambodia's horrific recent history is still tangibly felt today. An entire generation were forced to grow up too fast in a post-genocide world. Without the generation above to guide them, many have grown up with a skewed view of life and of childhood. Sadly, as a result, Cambodia is home to some of the most horrific child trafficking in our world today.

BIBLE VERSE

'The wrath of God is being revealed from heaven against all the godlessness and wickedness of people, who suppress the truth by their wickedness'
(Rom. 1:18).

REFLECTION

As we reflect on the history of Cambodia, both recent and more distant, we get a picture of a people and place sorely in need of redemption. For hundreds of years, the land switched between two equally false religions, with Angkor Wat standing as testament to the nation's ignorance of the one true God. More recently, some of the very worst acts mankind is capable of have been committed here, with millions imprisoned and executed simply because of who they were. We cannot truly comprehend the horror of the Pol Pot regime. This land is home to much godlessness and wickedness against which the wrath of God is a very pressing reality. Cambodia needs the healing, hope and redemption that only Christ can bring.

PRAYER

Lord, I pray for the land of Cambodia. I pray that many people here would repent of their sinful ways and begin to follow You. I thank You for those who are at work proclaiming Your message of forgiveness and restoration, and ask that You would work in the hearts of many unbelievers. Lord, please be with those who have suffered the acts of evil perpetuated here. May they know the comfort, healing and hope which only You can bring.

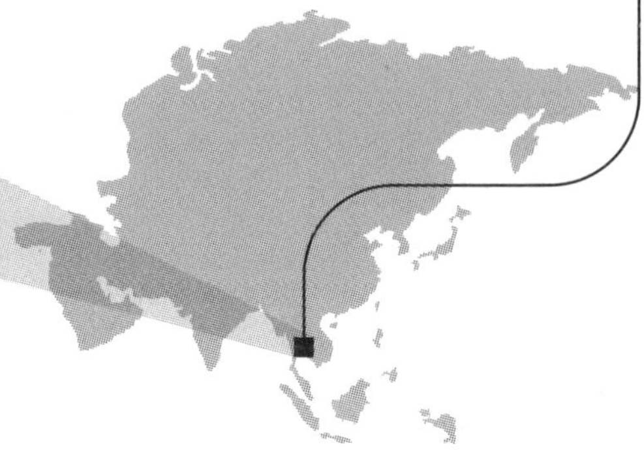

CAMBODIA

Part 2

On an evening walk along the streets of Phnom Penh, you are confronted with what must be one of the darkest and most evil places in the world. You have heard and read about it, but nothing prepares you for the realities of child exploitation.

The rich lawyer exercises in a main street gym just yards away from a woman who sits on a small sheet of cardboard. This is her home. Beside her is a home-made broom which she uses to sweep away the surrounding debris. Then, around the corner, you stumble upon a street where Western men sit outside cafes with young boys dressed in American baseball caps and Western clothes – all purchased, like their bodies, by their benefactors. These men shamelessly pour their pounds and dollars into an economy which turns a blind eye to the exploitation, degradation and even killing of children.

On the pavement sits a young woman, cradling her baby, while a toddler with blonde hair sits at her feet. Standing beside them is a girl, perhaps six years old, dressed in a white dress to represent her purity. Her eyes are downcast and resigned. There is no 'for sale' sign, but she will earn money tonight. Her mother shows no signs of regret or anxiety at her plight, having experienced the same ordeal just a few years ago. The children sitting around her are the product of that painful transaction. Shaken to your core, you turn away and cry out to God against the wickedness you have encountered. This area is known as the Heart of Darkness, and it has more than lived up to its name.

BIBLE VERSE

'The people walking in darkness have seen a great light; on those living in the land of deep darkness a light has dawned' (Is. 9:2).

REFLECTION

No longer can we turn a blind eye to the plight of children like these in Cambodia, who are so dearly loved by God. We must be deeply grateful for those who devote their lives to lovingly seeking them out, rescuing as many as they can and bringing them to a place of safety and security. Finding comfort in the words of Isaiah, we long for the day when the light of the Lord dispels the evil here in the Heart of Darkness. May the Lord raise up more passionate, godly men and women to fight this rampant exploitation and abuse, and use them to bring forgotten children like these into His glorious light. It is only through this light that these broken lives will know true healing and restoration.

PRAYER

Lord, I mourn the heartbreaking evil which takes place on a daily basis in Phnom Penh. Please bring about Your justice. Please put an end to the evils of human trafficking, child labour and sexual exploitation. Lord, I ask that You would be with those ministering in this area. Please lead and guide them, and use their efforts to rescue and redeem these beloved children of Yours. Lord, please open my eyes more and more to the evil in this world, that I might act justly and seek the good of the oppressed.

DAY 41

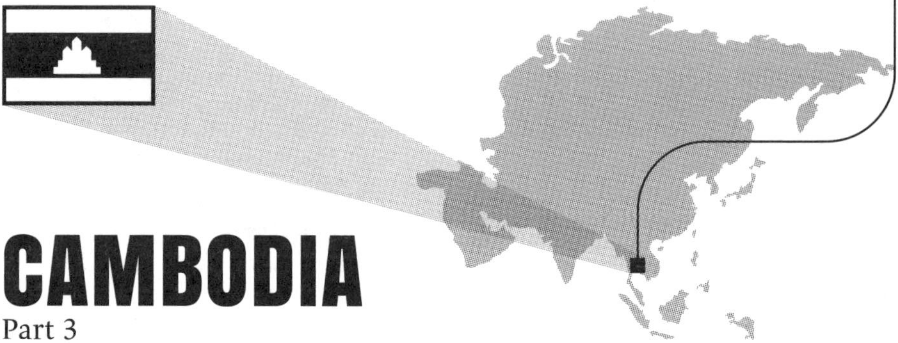

CAMBODIA
Part 3

Although every fibre of your being fights against it, you return to the Heart of Darkness this evening. The brazenness of the sordid activities is something you struggle to comprehend. Sex trafficking and prostitution do not only happen behind closed doors. At the front of every bar, there are women and children dancing provocatively, while men – both local and Western – approach girls of all ages and lead them away by the hand. How can such a place exist? How is this abuse allowed to continue?

You have not returned alone. Tonight, you are accompanied by some local believers who seek to reach and rescue those involved in the city's sex trade. It is difficult, emotionally draining work. The team have spent many hours building friendships with those being exploited here. They know everyone's story and catch up in the bars with them. Alcohol is free-flowing, the music is deafening and men with ill intent surround them, yet team members persist in conversation with these girls. The biggest challenge they face is that some girls do not see their need for help. Having been raised in this environment and lived like this for many years, they do not recognise how degrading and dark their plight is. They have never known anything else. For others, this life is preferable to the poverty they have escaped.

After much time, a great deal of prayer and many conversations, girls and women are encouraged to leave the sex industry. The team offer them training in jewellery making and take opportunities to introduce them to Christ. You leave Cambodia deeply burdened for the situation here, yet incredibly thankful for those working to see these girls restored to a life full of dignity, value and love.

BIBLE VERSE

*'The light shines in the darkness,
and the darkness has not overcome it'*
(John 1:5).

REFLECTION

It is tempting to think that there is no hope for places as evil and depraved as the Heart of Darkness. It is a place where the poor are oppressed and the vulnerable are downtrodden. With such an extensive spread of prostitution and sex trafficking, and such a broken, godless culture, the challenge is immense. But even in the darkness, the light is shining. John reminds us of the light which cannot be overcome by darkness – our Lord and Saviour Jesus Christ. He is the light of the nations, and that light is beginning to shine here in Cambodia through these outreach teams. Their work is slow and hard, and they are only able to scratch the surface of the problem. However, girls are coming out of the darkness into His glorious light, and every soul that is rescued and restored to relationship with the Father is a cause for great rejoicing.

PRAYER

Lord, I praise You that You are the light of the world! Darkness cannot overcome You, the gates of hell cannot prevail against You, and You even defeated death itself when You were raised! I pray that Your glorious light would shine brightly through the outreach teams in the Heart of Darkness. Please bring many girls out of the sex industry. Open their eyes to the depraved nature of their dark situation and to the life found in Jesus, the light of the world.

DAY 42

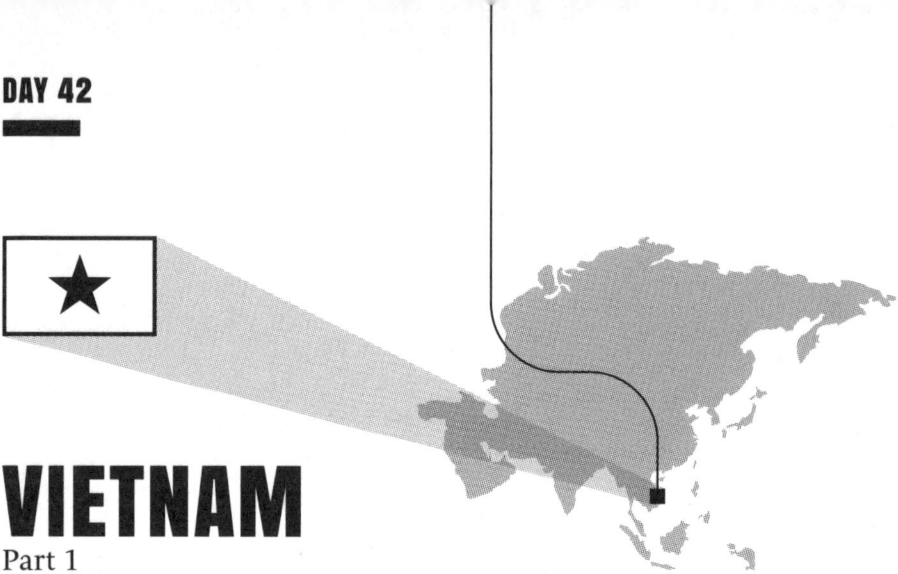

VIETNAM

Part 1

You arrive in Ho Chi Minh City, formerly known as Saigon. The humidity of the afternoon is stifling. You also find yourself in the moped capital of the world. With the roads fast and full, it seems impossible to navigate them safely! This is a popular tourist destination, attracting those who enjoy both the French architecture of colonial times as well as the impressive skyscrapers which would not look out of place in large Western cities. You settle into your modest but clean hotel. As evening approaches, you decide to take your life in your hands, using local transport to find a restaurant and visit one of the bustling markets. The city is filled with light, and the noise pollution from both humans and vehicles almost makes you wish you had stayed in and ordered room service!

In the 65 years since the North Vietnamese conquered this city, evangelical churches have slowly sprung up, giving an outward impression that the government is open to the Christian faith. However, when travelling to the provinces where ethnic minorities make up the population, it is an entirely different scenario. Here, churches face severe persecution, with pastors regularly tortured and imprisoned for their faith. For many, finding Christ means exile from family. In cases where a whole family comes to faith, they can find themselves thrown out of homes, schools and jobs, making it difficult to survive. However, many freed from animist practices into new life in Christ profess that the persecution they now suffer is no worse than their previous state. And wonderfully they no longer live in bondage to fear of every kind of spirit. Instead, the Holy Spirit lives within them!

BIBLE VERSE

'For the Spirit God gave us does not make us timid, but gives us power, love and self-discipline'
(2 Tim. 1:7).

REFLECTION

Consider the differences that exist between the regions of this beautiful country. In the provinces, there is little freedom of expression or worship; yet in the cities, there would appear to be a tolerance. But, on reflection, perhaps there is just a hairsbreadth between them, and at any time the tide could turn either way. As Christians, we should guard against becoming complacent in our faith and taking for granted our freedom to express ourselves in worship. Social and spiritual dangers remain for those within the cities who are relatively untouched by persecution, and they learn much as they hear of the trials endured by their provincial brothers and sisters.

PRAYER

Father, You are a generous and a merciful God. Thank You that in the struggles I face, Your Spirit dwells and is at work within me. Thank You that Your gifts of power, love and self-discipline are available to use for Your honour and glory. I pray that You would daily grant these gifts to Your people in Vietnam as they face social and spiritual opposition to their faith. Please help me not to take for granted the freedoms I have, but to live out the gospel each day with urgency and with a thankful heart.

DAY 43

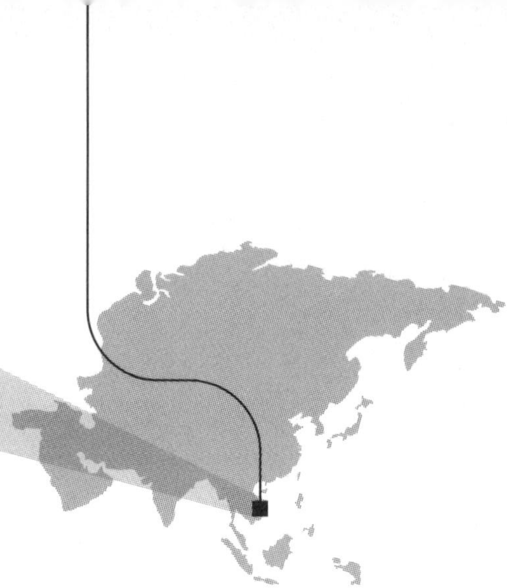

VIETNAM

Part 2

As morning dawns, you hear the invasive noise of unrelenting traffic and a sea of people making their way to work in this vibrant city. Today, you will begin a journey into the highlands of this amazing country. That in itself will be an adventure, but you are most excited to see how God is at work among the marginalised. You make the journey on a bus which stops countless times to drop off and pick up people and produce, both alive and dead. This country has seen so much war and devastation and, like other countries in Southeast Asia, the people in outlying areas are poor. Often, there are no running water, electricity or toilet facilities, and over 50 of the nation's 118 people groups remain unreached.

When you eventually arrive at your destination, you meet two dear people who are passionate about sharing the gospel of Christ with two of the most marginalised groups in Vietnam. They greet you with smiling faces and begin to tell you the story of how God is using them to reach many children in this area. They can only come occasionally because finances restrict their ability to travel. But when they do come, they share simple stories of Jesus and do basic craft with the children. This is making a huge difference in these young lives. There is a great harvest to be brought in here, but the workers and the resources are few.

They would like to provide Bibles for all the children in their heart language. Though it is possible to buy them, they are very expensive. A children's Bible would be even better, but at present there is no such version available.

BIBLE VERSE

'At that time Jesus said, "I praise you, Father, Lord of heaven and earth, because you have hidden these things from the wise and learned and revealed them to little children"' (Mt. 11:25).

REFLECTION

Jesus made it clear to His disciples how much He loved and valued children. There are parts of our world where children are seen as a commodity to be exploited or sold. In chapter 10 of Mark's Gospel, we read of Jesus' indignation when the disciples tried to prevent the little ones having access to Him. Children are still important to Him, and their ability to accept the simple truth that God loves them should encourage us to share that truth with them. How often do we take that opportunity in our own families, churches and communities?

PRAYER

Gracious Heavenly Father, please help me to share the good news of salvation with the children who are part of my life. I also pray for the children in Vietnam. In Your great love and mercy, please provide the resources needed to produce children's Bibles in their heart languages, that they might read Your Word and become increasingly rooted in the wonderful truths of the gospel.

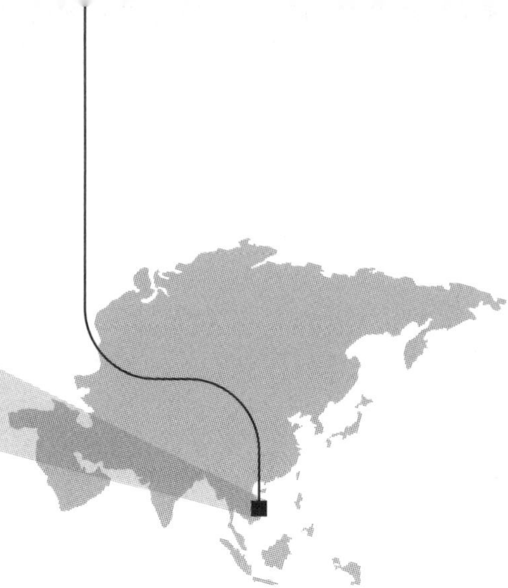

VIETNAM

Part 3

It is a still morning as you arrive in the north of the country. The mist hangs low over the trees and the view over the rice terraces reminds you again how different rural life is from that in the city. People here continue to use ancient methods to plant and harvest, making daily food supplies incredibly difficult and time-consuming to obtain. As tourism begins to grow in this area, some people groups are becoming increasingly able to trade craft work. Meanwhile, homestays have become a part of the new economy. Life is changing, but slowly.

Today, you meet a man who is short in stature, but this belies the largeness of his heart and his great love for the lost! Huy is one of those within this beautiful country who have recognised God's call on their lives and are working, with limited resources and finance, to bring the gospel to minority groups. Within the central highlands, there are many hill tribes, all of whom have different languages and dialects. Discipling new believers is difficult when only a fraction of your listeners understand Vietnamese! Huy works tirelessly to correct that, teaching, training and making God's Word available in the heart languages of many people groups. Sometimes the work is done through the written word; sometimes through audio resources. Both methods take time, energy and financial support.

Many of those served by this work have been saved from the bondage of animism. They have turned from an anxious fear of the spirits to certain hope in Christ. It can take a long time to teach them of our assurance as believers – that forgiveness is certain and our inheritance is guaranteed – but the Word of the Lord is mightily changing hearts across this nation.

BIBLE VERSE

'Show me your ways, Lord, teach me your paths. Guide me in your truth and teach me, for you are God my Saviour, and my hope is in you all day long'
(Ps. 25:4–5).

REFLECTION

How frustrated would you become if the Bible you possessed was written in a language you barely understood? How quickly would you learn its truths? How difficult might it be to stay the course? We often have many versions of the Bible in our possession, most of which will sit on the shelf gathering dust. How often do you take the time to read God's Word? And how often do you go deeper in study, using the many resources available in the English language? Hearing of those who do not share our access to Scripture must lead us to thankfulness for this blessing, joy in the Scriptures and a longing to see them shared in every language in the world.

PRAYER

Heavenly Father, thank You for men like Huy who are prepared to give their time and energy to help new believers access Your word in their own language. Thank You that although this ministry can at times be life-threatening, Huy's vision to see the Bible translated and distributed is coming to fruition. Please forgive me when I become casual about reading and studying Your Word, and when I take for granted my freedom even to own a Bible. Like the psalmist, please enable me to hide Your Word in my heart and hope in You all day long.

DAY 45

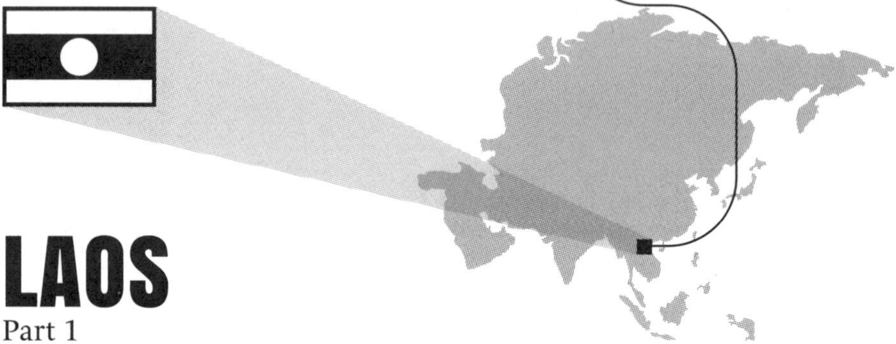

LAOS

Part 1

Today, you travel to the beautiful nation of Laos – the only landlocked country in Southeast Asia. It is home to over 130 people groups and around 70 different languages are spoken. The mighty Mekong River arrives from the plateaus of Tibet, meandering through the north-west of the country before forming a border with Thailand, then continuing through Vietnam and into the South China Sea. The capital, Vientiane, is the smallest in Southeast Asia. Like other cities in the nation, it features French colonial architecture, most of which is crumbling and in great need of repair. Nearby, the mountain and jungle regions are full of people groups residing in homes constructed from bamboo and topped with tin roofs. While Buddhism is accepted and remains the predominant religion, the Communist Party rules with an iron fist and Christians are regularly persecuted for their faith.

You are surprised to discover that it is the most bombed country in history, with over two million tonnes of bombs dropped here during the Vietnam War. On arrival at the border, there is an eery and unnerving quiet. You sense the invisible oppression which exists in this beautiful country as you approach the counter for a visa. Showing your passport and paying the $35 fee, taking great care to break no rules, you are relieved when your passport is stamped! Next, you journey on to the tiny city of Luang Prabang, passing the terraced rice paddies which provide a large proportion of the rural diet. You arrive at your hotel acutely aware that the authorities know exactly where to find you, should they wish, over the few days in which you will stay in Laos.

BIBLE VERSE

'For since the creation of the world God's invisible qualities – his eternal power and divine nature – have been clearly seen, being understood from what has been made, so that people are without excuse'
(Rom. 1:20).

REFLECTION

The Lao government denies the existence of God. They oppress and persecute those who follow Jesus, denying them basic human rights and the ability to live within their chosen communities. Yet all around them in this beautiful country is the evidence of a Creator God and His power. Paul talks in the verses preceding Romans 1:20 of a time when God will pour out His wrath on men 'who suppress the truth by their wickedness'. He makes it clear that no excuses will be accepted from those who fail to worship the Lord, because all around them lies evidence of His existence. Today, take some time to reflect on God's creation around you, whether it be a mountain, a park or a simple plant or tree. Ask Him to show you new things about Himself.

PRAYER

Gracious God, thank You that You made the heavens, the earth and everything within it. Please open the eyes of the Lao government and those who persecute Your people. Help them see who You are in the majestic creation around them. Give them a desire to know more about the creation and its Creator, and faith to believe. Please enable me to see new things about You today too, and cause me to give thanks that Your eternal power and divine nature are seen in all You have made.

DAY 46

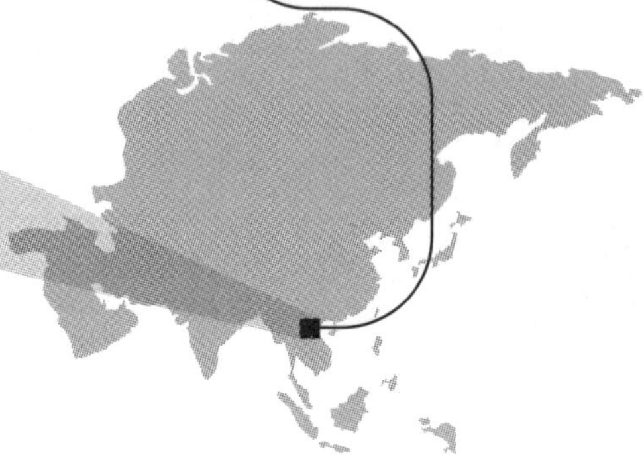

LAOS

Part 2

This morning, as you watch from the balcony of your hotel, long canoes negotiate the Nam Khan River. You feel like you are in a forgotten world: the pace of life is slow, with no hurry and low noise levels – other than the motorbikes upon which boy racers dart along the riverfront from time to time. People pass by, going about their business with solemnity. You spot a notice pinned on the wall just outside your bedroom – a reminder that it is unlawful to proselytise. You are aware that there are eyes everywhere watching, taking notes and doing their national duty.

You are approached by a Western man with a huge grin who introduces himself – his name is Simon. He explains his heart to reach the poorest of the poor in this land, helping them to provide their families with the basic necessities of daily life, while at the same time introducing them to the Lord Jesus. He has pioneered nine or ten different projects here, each ministering to villagers in remote areas. His heart exudes love for these dear, forgotten people.

Simon takes you on a journey outside of the city limits, to the farm where it all began. As you climb down from his vehicle, you are approached shyly by some little children with smiling faces who are intrigued by your appearance. Simon shows you a small piece of land where food production takes place, then a series of small, dark buildings where mushrooms grow. The products grown here are used to provide a better quality of diet and lifestyle for the rural poor, while using every opportunity to gently introduce these people to Jesus.

BIBLE VERSE

'Each of you should give what you have decided in your heart to give, not reluctantly or under compulsion, for God loves a cheerful giver'
(2 Cor. 9:7).

REFLECTION

The poor are all around us – everywhere we look – should we choose to see them. As you reflect on your journey today, you cannot help but be overwhelmed by Simon's love and care for the poorest people in Laos. His enthusiasm and absolute passion for providing basic help and care for those less fortunate than him is overwhelming. He gives of his time and his resources to bring the aid which so many here need, and so many elsewhere go without on a regular basis. With the provision of that aid, he is the hands and feet of the Lord Jesus. He gives from a heart full of what he has been given in order to see the kingdom of God lived out in this forgotten country. May we be inspired to follow his example of cheerful generosity!

PRAYER

Lord God, help me to reflect on the blessings which are mine: my home, my health, my family, my job. Help me recognise that You have given all of it, and it is all Yours. Please give me a compassionate heart which reaches out in love to those in need, both physically and spiritually. Help me to be a cheerful giver, freely sharing all I have been given with those in need. Thank You for Jesus, Your indescribable gift. Help me to express my thanksgiving to You through giving, and so to share in the ministry of the Lord Jesus.

DAY 47

LAOS

Part 3

The journey is dusty and bumpy as you travel up the steep mountain path to a village where the air is cooler but life is hard. Climbing higher and higher, you are increasingly overcome by the majestic mountains and the red and white poinsettias growing like giant trees on the hillsides. The number of avocados growing on the trees astounds you and does not prepare you for the level of poverty on display when you reach the village. You see a horse corralled in a small, makeshift stable and notice how thin he is. A friendly man seated outside on a doorstep rises to bring a chair for you, and you watch him stripping bamboo to make baskets. Pieces of cut paper hang from the doorframe – your driver explains they are there to ward off evil spirits.

As you move around the village, children appear from everywhere. Their little faces and hands are dirty, but they are full of mischief too. You reach into your bag for some sweets and a number of hands eagerly stretch out to accept these small gifts you have brought. You also discover the importance of a local project where young women are taught basic craft, sewing and beauty skills, which they then take back to their villages to supplement their family's income. This makes such a difference for these women, and for their families who no longer fear having to traffic their daughters in order to survive. You give thanks for those who saw such a need and had the vision and energy to meet it, and for God's grace allowing this work to flourish in such a restrictive nation.

BIBLE VERSE

'The Lord is my light and my salvation – whom shall I fear? The Lord is the stronghold of my life – of whom shall I be afraid?' (Ps. 27:1).

REFLECTION

The spiritual strongholds in the rural villages of Laos are deeply embedded and cause great anxiety. The darkness and oppression in which people live is palpable, and the way in which the enemy has bound them contributes to their poverty. Jesus wants to be their stronghold. He brings light into darkness, life from death, freedom to the captive. Why not examine your own life today, asking God to reveal to you the strongholds of your life and where the enemy has held you captive? Ask Him to free you and, by the power of His Holy Spirit, pour in the light of life who is Jesus. Those who minister in areas where there are demonic strongholds seek to bring not only food and dignity but also light and salvation. Why not ask God how you could bring His blessing to others, both near and far, for His glory and honour?

PRAYER

Gracious and loving God, thank You that because of Jesus' sacrificial death on Calvary's cross, I do not need to fear anything. Thank You that He broke the power of sin, death and hell, and that a way has been made to know freedom from captivity and release from fear. As Your servants minister in rural areas of Laos, where enemy strongholds are prevalent, please protect them and keep them safe. Give them wisdom, discernment and the ability to reveal Your light and love to those who live in poverty of spirit.

DAY 48

LAOS

Part 4

In a small house in the suburbs of Vientiane, the capital city of this incredible country, you visit a tiny Lao lady with a huge, loving heart, and a group of girls whom she has rescued from a life of prostitution. The parents of these girls never imagined that their children would be sold into the sex industry by the glamorous woman with the expensive clothes and handbag. She had promised to take good care of their beautiful girls, finding them work in upmarket restaurants and enabling them to send home some much-needed cash to feed and clothe their families.

Among this group is a little girl. The house mother tells you she is just seven years old. You cringe at the thought of what this child has suffered at the hands of cruel men. But she is different in some ways to the others, who are all in their early teens. Her story, when told, reveals that when she was six years old, her parents recognised that she was ill and took her to a hospital. There, the doctor diagnosed her as being HIV positive. Her neighbour, in whose care she had been left one day, had raped her. Her parents, apparently now ashamed either of themselves or of their daughter, said they could not take her back. They fled the hospital, leaving her in the care of the doctor.

But God had a plan. This doctor was a Christian and knew of a safe house where God's love, care and compassion was poured out on broken, hurting girls. He knew she would find refuge there while receiving his continued medical attention, enabling her to overcome the trauma and loss of both her childhood and her family.

BIBLE VERSE

'Rescue me, Lord, from evildoers; protect me from the violent' (Ps. 140:1).

REFLECTION

In the West today, this scenario would be unthinkable. Any parent would want justice for this girl. We would seek to love, protect and restore her. In Laos, the shame brought on the parents was considered far more costly than disowning her, even though she was the victim. This challenges our own response to children engaging in activities we deem shameful, whether it be violence, drugs, sex or crime. Do we first seek to remove the plank from our own eye (Mt. 7:5), realising that we are in no position to throw the first stone (John 8:7)? Moreover, this situation raises questions about justice. In Psalm 140, David cried out for rescue from evildoers. But this was no cry of desperate hope, for David knew that the Lord secures justice for the poor and upholds the cause of the needy (v. 12). We can have confidence in God's justice, even in the midst of wickedness.

PRAYER

Gracious God and loving Heavenly Father, thank You that even though You know the intimate details of my heart and my life, You love me unconditionally. Thank You for those who minister that love to girls whom evil men have cruelly used and abused. Please empower Your servants and strengthen them for the task of rescue and restoration. Help me also today to minister acceptance and grace to those with whom I walk and talk.

DAY 49

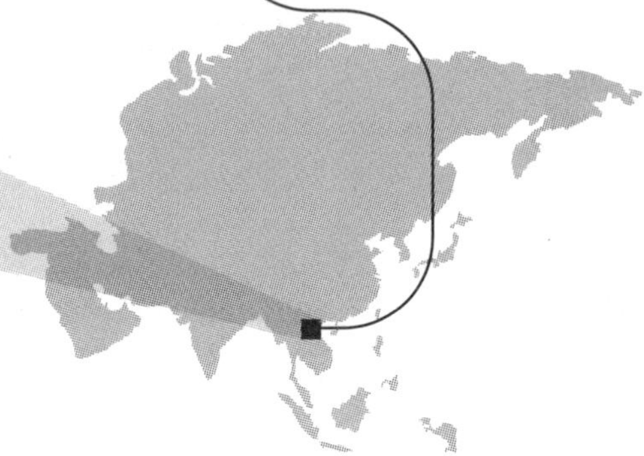

LAOS

Part 5

Before you head off on the next leg of the journey, you enjoy a cup of Lao coffee and a delicious pastry in a stylish coffee shop – one of the many indicators of French colonial history in this region. As you reflect on the conversation you had with the woman on the bus last night, you marvel at the ways in which God is using simple storytelling to reach the lost people of this country.

She had settled beside you, placing somewhere on the rack above a basket of goods she would no doubt sell in a market. She had a lovely smile and a soft voice as she greeted you. You tried to use some of the basic language skills you have picked up in your time here. As you conversed slowly and quietly, she took a book out of the bag draped around her. She opened it, revealing many pictures and little text, and you recognised the story of creation and the Garden of Eden. She began to tell the story. As you struggled to keep up with the language, you were glad that you knew it well! After a while, you asked who had given her this book and if she believed the stories within it. Her response affirmed that she was a Christian in a country where being so is difficult at best, and life-threatening at worst. Yet her passion is to share this story with others. She explained that most of her women friends cannot read or write, and so she uses this book to tell them stories about the love of God in Christ, who died for them.

BIBLE VERSE

'He told them many things in parables' (Mt. 13:3).

REFLECTION

Jesus Himself was the greatest storyteller. He explained to the uneducated people of His time the truth concerning His kingdom using stories. Who of us did not like to hear a story as a child? Most of us still love a good story even now! Have you ever reflected on how you could share the message of the gospel using stories? Could you be bold enough to sit next to somebody today and tell a story of Moses, or of David, or of Jesus to your neighbour sitting right beside you? We possess the greatest story ever told, but do we take every opportunity to share it with those who most need to hear?

PRAYER

Sovereign God, thank You that the people of Laos are being reached and saved through those who are bold enough to share the greatest story. Thank You for those who fearlessly declare Your love in Christ to those who are lost. Please use them to bring many into Your kingdom! Please also give me boldness to reach out to those with whom I come in contact and to share the story, just as Jesus did.

DAY 50

MYANMAR

Part 1

Sandwiched between two great neighbours in India and China lies Myanmar. It ranks in the bottom quarter of the World Development Index and has not experienced country-wide peace since independence in 1948. The population is over 80% Buddhist, with the central belt's ethnic Bamar people making up much of this number. Around the fringes of the Irrawaddy plain lie the hills of the minority groups, many of whom follow animist traditions, while others are Christian.

The task of reaching Myanmar's unreached people groups is central to the work of the theological college you are visiting. Located in the former imperial capital, Yangon, it trains and sends out future pastors and missionaries. As class begins, you watch proceedings. Students sit on green plastic chairs at desks, taking notes from the white board. It may not seem dramatic in the world's eyes, but what they learn today will be put into practice tomorrow and will reverberate into eternity. Later, you meet some students from different ethnic groups in remote areas. Their common language is Burmese, but few speak it as their mother tongue. You discover that some plan to go back to their homes to lead churches, while others will be sent out as pioneer missionaries, crossing yet another cultural divide even within the nation's borders.

You catch up with Brother Ko, who oversees the college and the network of hundreds of pastors sent out from here. He explains that the church is growing through their work across the country. Ko spends much of his time visiting the churches, encouraging and advising pastors as they share the joys and trials of ministry. His bold vision is that the work would grow and grow.

BIBLE VERSE

'Therefore I endure everything for the sake of the elect, that they too may obtain the salvation that is in Christ Jesus, with eternal glory'
(2 Tim. 2:10).

REFLECTION

Ministry for these young people involves sacrifice. First, they leave their homes, their families and their communities. They come to a large city they have never visited before and learn in a language they do not speak fluently. They must learn new ways of thinking, living, understanding the Bible and sharing the good news. Once trained, many are sent out to another unfamiliar place to reach people from another ethnic group and language who may reject and oppose them. Paul explains that for the unchanging gospel he was willing to endure everything for the sake of the elect. He faced dangers, robbers, beatings, slander and more, but willingly paid a personal price to hold out the news of salvation in Christ. His ministry was not always a bed of roses! These eager, young workers in Myanmar share Paul's mindset and are seeking to follow his example, whatever the cost.

PRAYER

Lord, I pray that the many ethnic groups in Myanmar would come to live together in harmony. I pray that the gospel of peace would advance through these young trainees. Keep them true to Your Word and give them joy, even as they make sacrifices to serve You and others. Give them boldness in witness and passion in preaching. Make them holy in conduct and blameless before outsiders. May their lives bear witness to Your Spirit's work in them, and may they see many come to saving faith in You.

DAY 51

MYANMAR

Part 2

Today, you drive north past rows of teak trees and occasional banyan. The humidity is rising but for now you delight in the sight of dark green forested hills on the skyline. You enter the village through a military checkpoint. The houses are constructed on sturdy teak stilts. The area below one house provides shelter at night for a brown zebu, with the living space accessed via a steep external staircase. Pastor Hla, his wife and their one-year-old daughter live here. They have a small adjoining bedroom. All of their possessions fit into a single metal trunk.

The church – several men, women and children – has gathered to meet and share a drink of tea with you. Some are fanning themselves. The small solar panel doesn't provide enough power for air conditioning, which is a costly luxury these villagers cannot afford. With Ko's help interpreting, you ask how the church came about.

'When we first came,' begins Hla, 'the people were not happy with us. They did not want to trade with us. Some said we should go away with our foreign God. Others threw stones at this house. Then we dedicated a well to God and invited all the people to hear about the living water of the Lord Jesus. Many people got sick before that, but it is better now. Anyone in the village can take the water and they became friendlier. We invited them to church and some came. Last year, a few of these men and their wives were baptised. They believed.'

'Is it easy to follow Jesus?' you ask.

'Still a few people make trouble, but most now accept us. Before, if something bad happened, like a crop failure, they said, "It is these Christians." But they don't say that much now. They like the clean water. And,' Hla laughs, 'some like Jesus too.'

BIBLE VERSE

'On the last and greatest day of the festival, Jesus stood and said in a loud voice, "Let anyone who is thirsty come to me and drink"'
(John 7:37).

REFLECTION

Often in Myanmar, the barrier of prejudice needs to be broken down so that the gospel can get a hearing. One of the biggest needs in rural areas is access to clean water – without it, people get sick and can even die. We know that Jesus is the source of spiritual life for everyone. We need to come to Jesus, to trust Him, to satisfy our spiritual thirst and to receive the life He gives by the Spirit. The yearning of the people is evident – there are shrines to Buddha all over this land. But Buddha cannot give the life-giving water. Only Jesus can meet the craving of each heart.

PRAYER

Lord Jesus, You alone are the true source of living water that springs up to eternal life. Please give this water to the people of Myanmar. Let the trickle of springs become a life-giving flood over the land. Let Your healing be a balm to this divided and parched land. Let Your kingdom come and Your name be lifted high above the idols. Let them be a missionary-sending church. May they find Your living water to be ever-refreshing, and let it flow out of them in turn as a blessing to those they meet.

DAY 52

MYANMAR

Part 3

Much further north along the border with Thailand lies a very different picture of everyday life for the people of Myanmar. A two-hour journey by road brings you to a little clearing in the jungle by the side of a wide, muddy river. Here, a small community has grown up over the past 15 years – made up primarily of children who are the product of a war which has raged for the past 60 years. Some of these children arrived at this safe place after walking many days, or even months. Many have witnessed the brutal killing of their parents and other family members, along with the destruction of their villages and homes. Such harrowing experiences are what caused them to flee into the jungle in fear of being conscripted into the attacking army, or worse.

As your truck, driven by Mommy Paw, pulls into the compound, the children come running out of the little tin-roofed building which has a cross mounted on the apex. They hug Mommy Paw, and you too as you step down onto the dry and dusty driveway! Some of them are wearing thanaka on their faces. Several have applied it with great care, creatively drawing animal faces on their own. You are overwhelmed by the heat, but more so by the love which pours from each little face gazing up into your own.

Refugees from Myanmar number over 130,000 and are situated in a number of camps along the border with Thailand. They have no status and no rights to education or work outside of the camps in which they live. They receive minimal health care and there seems to be little prospect of their lot ever improving.

BIBLE VERSE

'The Lord builds up Jerusalem; he gathers the exiles of Israel. He heals the broken-hearted and binds up their wounds' (Ps. 147:2–3).

REFLECTION

These verses speak hope into the hearts of God's people and this hope is what the believers working in these areas are attempting to share, particularly with the refugee children. All of them have broken hearts from the death and destruction they have witnessed, resulting in wounds which need to be bound. They need to see their families rebuilt wherever possible, and are desperate to be returned from exile in a strange and foreign land. More than anything, they need to know the saving and healing power of Jesus Christ. This psalm portrays the Lord as gently administering healing and restoration. Such a way of life is produced by the Spirit. Mommy Paw's team of godly believers minister that gentle care and healing here, longing to show the love of God to these broken little ones.

PRAYER

Sovereign Lord, I praise You that You are good and great. Thank You that You know and care intimately for each of the little exiled souls in Myanmar's refugee camps. Thank You for those who share the love of the Lord Jesus with them in tenderness and compassion. Please enable each young person to experience Your healing, restoration and love as Mommy Paw and her team minister to them in the power of Your Holy Spirit.

DAY 53

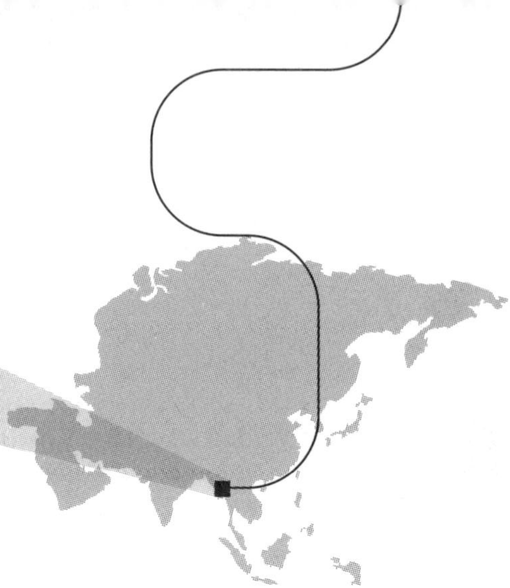

MYANMAR

Part 4

In the grey light of dawn, a chicken squawks before an axe hits wood. This poor creature will be your breakfast. Last night, you stayed in this remote place with a pastor who cares for 40 orphans in a refugee camp housing over 20,000 people. There is no electricity, save an occasional burst from the generator, so night-time toilet visits require a headtorch. Slippery, eight-inch planks lead to a little shack enclosing a hole to squat over … and a large spider! You decide that, given the choice, you would prefer to take your chances with the elephant which had appeared the day before as you journeyed up the mountain!

Before daybreak, you join with the children and the medical team in worship. A family of five children shuffle in nervously, led by a girl of around 11 years. They arrived at the camp the previous night having fled their village over two months ago when the Burmese army attacked. Their father was murdered during the assault. Then, as they fled, their mother was killed by a landmine and their aunt blinded. In desperation, this young girl left her aunt and baby sister in the hands of others in order to escort her other siblings to the camp. The trauma is visibly etched onto the face of each of these dirty, malnourished children. The team doctor checks them over before they are taken away by the pastor's wife to be bathed and dressed in clean clothes. You spend the day helping to administer vitamins, painkillers, and worm and lice treatments to hundreds of people arriving at the makeshift clinic. Come the end of the day, you reflect on God's goodness to you and ponder, 'Why me and not them?'

BIBLE VERSE

'I form the light and create darkness, I bring prosperity and create disaster; I, the Lord, do all these things' (Is. 45:7).

REFLECTION

Sometimes, we wrestle with the difficult question of why some people prosper while bad things happen to the innocent. In the preceding verses of Isaiah 45, we encounter Cyrus. This ruler did not acknowledge the Lord (vv. 4–5), but was used by Him to set the exiles free. Isaiah reveals that God is sovereign over not just those who acknowledge Him, but also those who do not, whether through ignorance or by deliberate choice. God's sovereignty enables us to trust Him with the plight of those who are oppressed and afflicted. The question 'Why them and not me?' will remain unanswered this side of glory. Rather, let us look at how God has blessed us, then seek to bless those who are in the midst of pain and suffering – helping, aiding and encouraging them in the Lord.

PRAYER

Lord, thank You that You know the answers to difficult questions. It seems like innocent children are often caught in destruction, but I thank You that even when all seems hopeless, You are in control. Thank You for those who willingly give of their time and their talents to minister to these refugees. Please forgive me when I use what You have given me frivolously, and remind me that all I have is Yours. You have given it to me for Your glory – please help me to use what I have to bless those who need it most.

DAY 54

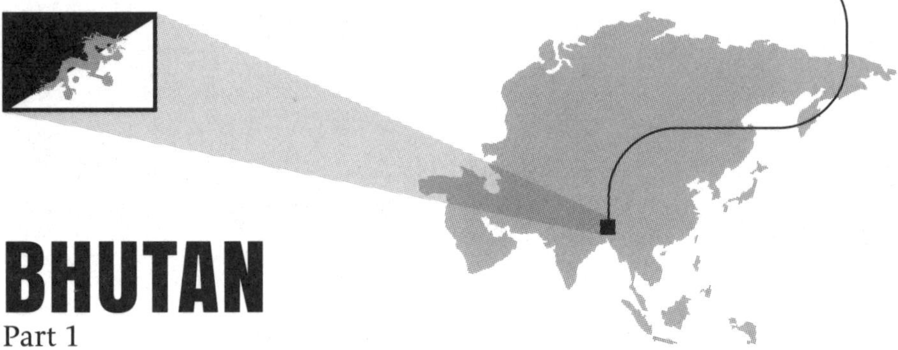

BHUTAN

Part 1

The flight into Paro is a journey like no other, offering the rare opportunity to see the colossal Himalayan mountains from above. Like many others, you reserved seats on the left side of the plane and so enjoy breathtaking aerial views of Everest and K2 before the steep descent into Paro, the plane weaving through a valley before touching down on a runway cut startlingly short by the side of a mountain. It is an unforgettable introduction to an unforgettable nation.

Nestled high in the Himalayas, Bhutan is the last Buddhist kingdom on earth. The mountainous scenery and ornate buildings are stunning, yet few have explored this small nation. Nicknamed the Hermit Kingdom, the country was extremely resistant to outsiders until recent times. Foreign influences are now creeping in, slowly, as tourism is increasingly encouraged.

You soon discover that to be Bhutanese is to be Buddhist. This is a core part of the national identity. Bhutan is also the only nation which measures Gross National Happiness, considering itself the happiest nation on earth. However, digging a little deeper reveals a profound sadness perpetuated by a works-based religion offering no hope, no assurance and no salvation. Nowhere is this more evident than in the capital, Thimpu, where the National Memorial Stupa – a mammoth white monument – is visible from across the city. Around the stupa stomp scores of Buddhist worshippers utilising prayer beads and prayer wheels. To one side, men bow fervently in prayer, the wood beneath them rubbed smooth by their repeated diving actions. Elderly men and women around the stupa are particularly desperate in prayer, longing that their next life might be better than this. Your heart breaks as the scene plays out. How many like them have done this before and passed away without ever hearing the gospel?

BIBLE VERSE

'The fear of the Lord leads to life; then one rests content, untouched by trouble'
(Prov. 19:23).

REFLECTION

It is particularly ironic that a country measuring Gross National Happiness prizes the Buddhist faith as an integral part of its national identity. The desperate sight of elderly men and women in fearful prayer attests that life as a Buddhist can bring neither true happiness nor contentment. This verse in Proverbs reminds us that there is only one source of true contentment. Only when we fear the Lord and believe in His Son do we receive the new life of joy and contentment. Only then can we rest in the assurance, regardless of trials and tribulations, of a blessed today and a better tomorrow. Let us approach the Lord not in fear of death or judgment, but in the fear which leads to that glorious life – life to the full – promised by God's own Son Himself (John 10:10).

PRAYER

Lord, I praise You for the deep contentment which is found in You alone. Please help me to know and experience that truth more deeply each day. Thank You that when I turn my eyes to You, the cares and worries of this life can melt away. Lord, I pray that the people of Bhutan would come to know You as their eternal source of happiness and contentment. May their eyes be opened to the emptiness of false religion, and may their hearts turn gladly to You in the certain hope of peace.

DAY 55

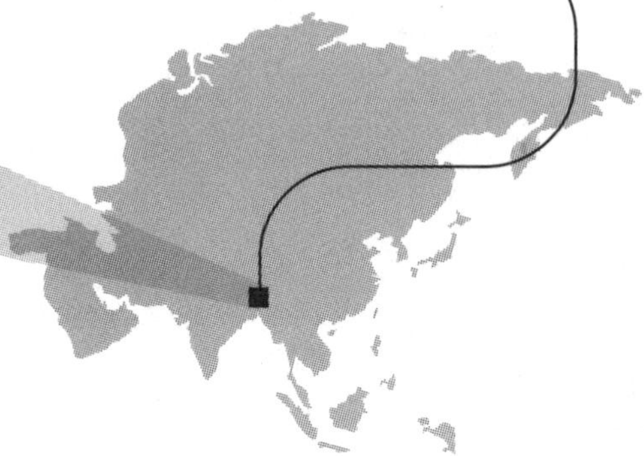

BHUTAN

Part 2

In Bhutan's capital, Thimpu, you meet with a house church and learn of the difficulties they face. Unable to own land collectively, they cannot build churches or bury loved ones who pass away. Churches meet in homes and risk being shut down if neighbours complain to the authorities. There are anti-conversion laws too, making it extremely difficult to share the gospel. Those who break these laws may be stripped of citizenship, thus losing access to employment, education and healthcare. Despite all this, you learn that the church continues to grow!

The deep hunger for God's Word is palpable among these believers, with their faith evidently central to their identity. They seek a deep understanding of God's Word, asking many questions about the teaching they receive. Your host expresses his desire to train evangelists who can cautiously move throughout the country, sharing the gospel and seeing lives won for Christ.

You leave to undertake a precarious 12-hour journey along a mountainside road to meet with another fellowship. You do so under cover of darkness so as not to raise suspicion. Squeezed into two small rooms, the 50 members of this underground church have gathered from the surrounding area, some having travelled 30 miles on foot to be here. You are encouraged to see numerous young believers. God has moved in this area over the last few years and blessed the church with many converts, despite all the difficulties they face. One new believer is too afraid to tell her father as she's convinced he will beat her. Still, the young people here are passionate for evangelism and you are thrilled by their eagerness to reach friends, family and communities with the good news of Jesus Christ.

BIBLE VERSE

'He replied, "Blessed rather are those who hear the word of God and obey it"'
(Luke 11:28).

REFLECTION

What an encouragement the Bhutanese church are! They are tucked far away in the Himalayas, meeting in secret and yet exhibiting a deep desire not only to delve into the truths of God's Word but also to see others come to know Christ as their Lord and Saviour. It is a wondrous thing that this is happening in a land where these believers are routinely discriminated against and evangelism is strictly forbidden. How amazing to learn of young people eager and willing to turn to Christ, living and witnessing for Him. These are believers earnestly seeking to obey God's Word and truly knowing the Lord's blessing. Will we too be people who hear and obey the Word, living out the life-changing news of the gospel and seeking to make Christ's name known to those around us?

PRAYER

Lord, thank You for the encouragement of these churches in Bhutan. Thank You for raising up a faithful body who witness in this hidden part of the world. Please bless and guide those who seek to make Your name known in Bhutan. I pray that You would use the Bhutanese church mightily, bringing many more to Yourself as these faithful believers boldly witness for You.

DAY 56

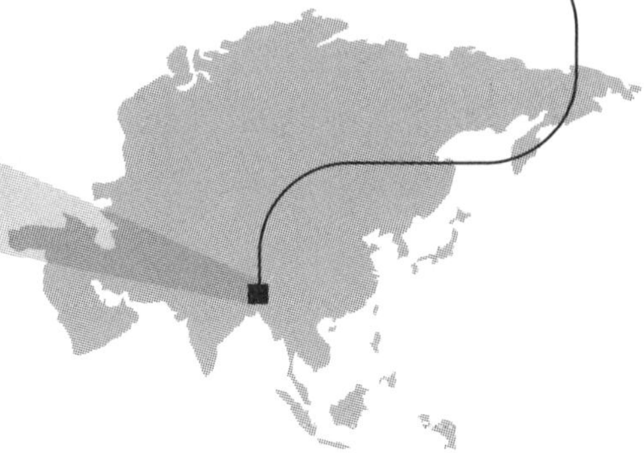

BHUTAN

Part 3

Bhutan is a small nation, home to only three quarters of a million people. Despite this, it is an incredibly diverse place with 76 different people groups represented. Most are Buddhist, with less than 1% of people having heard of Jesus.

Temples and pagodas populate the towns and cities, multi-coloured Buddhist prayer flags cover the whole country and there is no shortage of prayer wheels. Locals believe that by simply spinning the wheel they increase their chance of reaching nirvana – the ultimate goal of any Buddhist. It would be wrong to characterise nirvana as the Buddhist heaven; it is less a place of eternal rest and perfection, and more a place of annihilation where the Buddhist is thought to be finally released from the never-ending circle of reincarnation, ceasing to exist entirely.

Festivals take place throughout the year, usually centred around various religious beliefs. You stop in a town where one such festival is taking place. Before you, a drama – the Dance of the Judgement of the Dead – is unfolding before crowds of spectators. The performance features a man dancing around a fire, collecting both black and white stones. The white stones represent all his good deeds, while the black represent the bad. He eventually offers the stones to a monstrous figure – the Lord of the Dead – who proceeds to weigh them up. Eventually, this figure throws the stones into the fire – the man has not done enough good in his life and is thus condemned to rebirth in a Buddhist hell. This frightening performance reveals a disturbing reality: hundreds of thousands of people in Bhutan are seeking to earn their salvation, entirely unaware that our accumulation of 'black stones' can only be atoned for through faith in the cross of Christ.

BIBLE VERSE

'... while we were still sinners, Christ died for us' (Rom. 5:8).

REFLECTION

The performance of the Dance of the Judgement of the Dead is truly chilling. It dramatises what will happen to each and every person who tries to build up good works in order to justify themselves. It must make us grateful for all that the only true judge, our Lord, has graciously done for us. While we must all appear before the judgment seat of Christ, the Buddhist majority in Bhutan are desperately trying to collect those 'white stones', not knowing that before God they can never have enough. They have not heard or understood the good news that God has graciously given His Son to die for the ungodly, bearing the weight of the judgement we deserve. Through Him, we are saved from judgment and reconciled to God. Hallelujah!

PRAYER

Lord, it is so troubling to think about all those people in places like Bhutan who are desperately trying to gather up good works. I pray that they would come to know the forgiveness offered in Christ, through faith and by grace. Thank You for all You have done in saving me. Please help me, by Your Spirit, to rejoice in Your grace, to make others aware of the judgment that awaits us all, and to share the good news that salvation and reconciliation are found in Christ.

DAY 57

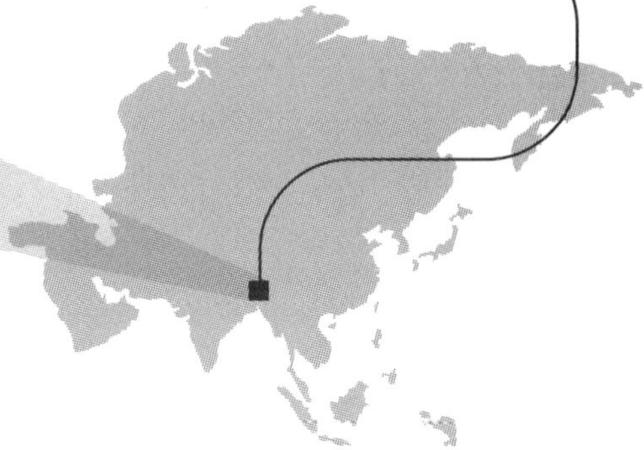

BHUTAN

Part 4

In another house church, you meet Pastor Tandin, whose deep passion for evangelism and discipleship strikes you. He spends most days sharing Christ. You sit transfixed as he tells the incredible story of his testimony.

As a young boy, Tandin was sent to train in a Buddhist monastery. It was a difficult experience. Older monks would abuse the boys, often in full view of outsiders. He remembers being scared and missing his family amid unfamiliar surroundings. He meditated on the teachings of Buddha for years as a monk, but the inner peace others described continued to evade him, causing constant torment. However, one night everything began to change. As he slept, a man dressed in white appeared and asked why he was troubled. Tandin explained his struggle. The man asked if he had told Jesus about these things. This unfamiliar name troubled him even more! He awoke determined to find out who this Jesus was.

Just a few days later, as he meditated in the park, an Indian man sat beside him. An expert in computers, he began to discuss technology with Tandin before asking, bluntly, 'Does Buddhism satisfy your deepest needs?' Tandin told the stranger of his dream and the constant struggle within. Amazingly, the man said he knew this Jesus and explained the gospel! Tandin was so excited to hear of the cross. He asked Jesus for forgiveness before returning to the monastery to proclaim the true peace found in Christ. Tandin laughs as he remembers being thrown out of the monastery! He maintained relationships with the monks and over time some others trusted in Jesus. He has since returned to the mountains to share the gospel there.

As you leave, you thank the Lord for Tandin. How wonderful and mighty is the Lord!

BIBLE VERSE

'... he saved us ... because of his mercy' (Tit. 3:5).

REFLECTION

Tandin's testimony is a wonderful story of the grace of God. How incredible that someone who was steeped in the teachings of Buddhism had such an amazing encounter with the Lord, leading to saving faith! It was such a transformation for Tandin to turn from a life as a Buddhist monk to follow Christ, later becoming a pastor and a passionate evangelist for the gospel. How great is our God! What an encouragement it is to know the Lord is still at work, saving souls and changing lives in places as far away as Bhutan! And none of this is achieved by purely human effort, but by the grace and mercy of God. Let us pray that God would keep bringing people to Himself in this mountain nation, whether through dreams and visions or through the hard work of His joyful servants.

PRAYER

Lord, thank You for Your amazing grace! Thank You that nobody is beyond Your reach – that even monks in Buddhist monasteries can be transformed by the good news of the gospel and sent out to serve for the glory of Your name! Lord, I thank You for Tandin, for his testimony and for the work he does for You. I pray that there would be many more stories of salvation as he and others like him continue to labour in Your harvest field in Bhutan.

DAY 58

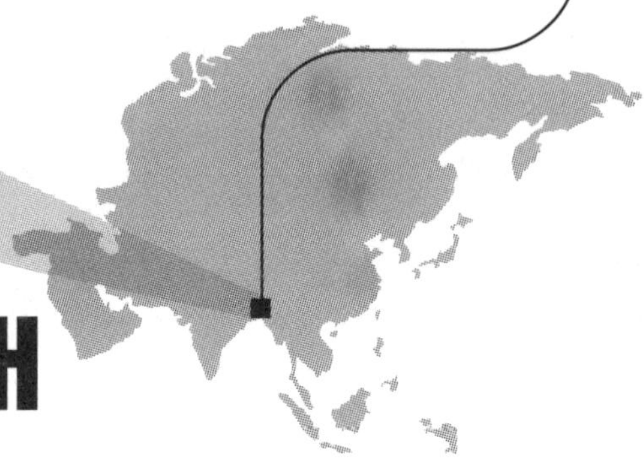

BANGLADESH

Part 1

People everywhere! That's what strikes you as you travel into the centre of Dhaka. You have read that this is the most densely populated city in the world, and it certainly looks like it from your vantage point in the back of the taxi. After checking into your hostel, you venture out to take in some of the city's sights and sounds. Unlike many other large cities in Asia, there is a noticeable absence of Western tourists. You soon become the centre of attention for the locals, with many stopping and staring as you leave the taxi. You spend some time walking the streets before a group of rickshaw drivers all jockey for your attention. It's not long before you're weaving through the crowds at breakneck speed on your way to the busiest market you have ever seen. After a while, you are glad to find a little tea stall where you can rest your legs and dip into the guide book.

Beyond the pictures of beautiful Bengal tigers and lists of other cultural highlights, you read that Bangladesh has had a turbulent political history. When the nation declared independence in 1971, its political instability was summed up by a former US president who labelled Bangladesh 'an international basket case'. Hinduism and Buddhism have both influenced Bangladesh, but the Muslim missionaries who arrived in the 12th century left a legacy which continues to define the country to this very day. On paper, Bangladesh is a secular state boasting freedom of religion, but Islam is established as 'the religion of the republic' and Muslims make up 90% of the population. However, you have heard there is a growing Christian community too and are looking forward to meeting some of them tomorrow.

BIBLE VERSE

'When Jesus heard what had happened, he withdrew by boat privately to a solitary place'
(Mt. 14:13).

REFLECTION

We all need solitude at times, some more than others depending on our personality types. In a place like Dhaka, it is very difficult to be alone and practically impossible to find a quiet place. Jesus faced a similar problem as His public ministry grew and crowds wanted to hear Him teach. Often He would deliberately remove Himself from the crowds in search of isolation and spend time alone with His Father. This is vital for us too, even though we neither have the following Jesus had nor live in such a busy place as Bangladesh. Why not carve out some space today to find a quiet place and be refreshed in the Lord's presence? You could also take some time to pray for the 160 million people in Bangladesh who are unreached by the gospel, and for the Christian workers seeking to witness to them.

PRAYER

Loving Father, thank You for the opportunity to spend time with You today. Please remind me day by day just how much I need these times in my Christian life. I pray for the people of Bangladesh, especially those facing unbearable hardship. Please bless the various Christian agencies who are working to alleviate suffering among those living in extreme poverty. And please move by Your Holy Spirit to raise up more evangelists and church planters to share the gospel among the 300 unreached people groups in Bangladesh. Build Your church here, Lord!

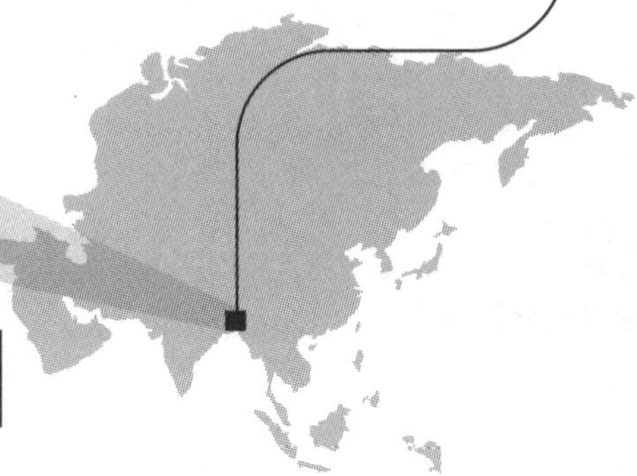

BANGLADESH

Part 2

All that you have heard about the dangerous roads appears to be true! Having seen several accidents today, you feel quite relieved as your bus arrives at the north-eastern city of Sylhet. Outside the bus station, you are met by a chaotic, colourful mess of cycle rickshaws. As soon as you make eye contact with one of the drivers, you climb onboard and make your way through a maze of narrow streets.

You have arranged to meet Faysal, one of the few evangelists working in the city, in a little shop where he sells mobile phone accessories. The locals here, like many other places in Asia, seem partial to attaching glittery bling to their phone cases! Faysal is a warm-faced man with a warm, engaging manner and a good grasp of English, so conversation flows easily. He tells you about his family and invites you to a meal in their home this evening, which a few others will join too.

As the visitors start to arrive at Faysal's home, it is not long before the cosy room is full, with people squeezing into every available space. After enjoying a most delicious curry, your host welcomes everyone and introduces tonight's study. The Bible is read and explained, and members of the group share thoughts and ask questions. Several have recently become Christians, while others are interested seekers who have been invited along after spiritual conversations in the phone shop. One young woman shares her story, explaining that she trusted Christ two years ago and has suffered intimidation and abuse by members of her extended family ever since. You get a deep sense that this little gathering is a lifeline, both for her and the other believers who meet here week by week.

BIBLE VERSE

'They broke bread in their homes and ate together with glad and sincere hearts' (Acts 2:46).

REFLECTION

After Peter preached the good news on the day of Pentecost, the Holy Spirit wonderfully moved and the Lord began to build His church. As we read of these early believers in the book of Acts, there appears to be a simplicity and authenticity about how they went about church life (vv. 42–47). In Bangladesh, as in many other Asian countries, the church often has a casual feel, where the focus is more on people than programmes or premises. Rich bonds of fellowship form in this atmosphere of love as believers share their lives together and build one another up in their faith. It is good for us to remember the small groups of Christians who gather in places like Sylhet, praying for them amid their struggles and reflecting on the lessons we can learn from their expressions of fellowship.

PRAYER

Loving Father, thank You for the fellowship I can enjoy with other Christians as we meet in church. Please help me to fully appreciate how blessed I am with so many opportunities to be encouraged in my faith. I pray for Christians in countries like Bangladesh who are in such a small minority, facing opposition and intimidation even from friends and family. Please bless pastors and evangelists in such places – give them grace and strength to serve You today, and encourage them as lost souls turn to Christ, repenting of sin and trusting Him as Saviour.

DAY 60

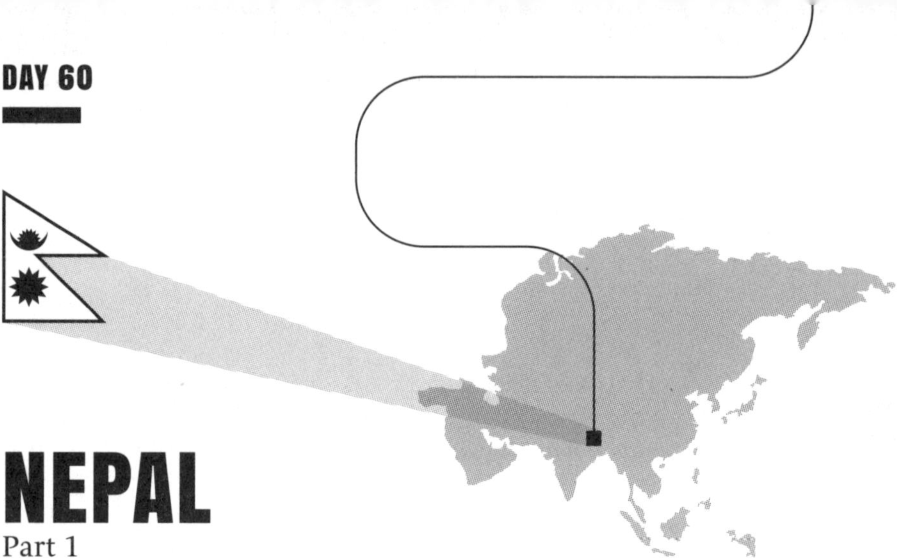

NEPAL

Part 1

Boarding your last connecting flight to Kathmandu, you have the golden ticket: a window seat on the left-hand side of the plane! This will give you a perfect view of the Himalayas, the rooftop of the world. You are not disappointed and find yourself rummaging around in your head for words to describe the vista. The best adjectives you can muster are 'majestic' and 'awesome', yet even these seem inadequate.

Stepping out of the airport, a sensory overload of sound and colour awaits, but it's the smell that hits you hardest. Wherever you go, it's impossible to escape the stench of burning. It's not long before you understand why. Kathmandu is sometimes called the city of temples, with Hindu and Buddhist places of worship everywhere you look. The northern Himalayan region is mostly Buddhist, but central and southern parts are strongly Hindu and make up 84% of the population. Although currently a secular state, a Hindu nationalist undercurrent is pushing for a return to the way things were prior to the abolition of the monarchy in 2006. As a result, Christians are facing increasing opposition.

Travelling around the city, evidence remains of the massive earthquake and aftershocks which rocked the entire region back in 2015, killing over 9000 people. Repairs to some of the world heritage sites, with their ornate architecture, will take years. Many streets are still surfaced with compacted rubble, making for a bumpy ride. It seems that every other westerner in your guesthouse has come to trek in the mountains, either along the Everest base camp route or through the Annapurna range. Though these mountains declare the glory of the Lord, so many in Nepal have yet to meet Him.

BIBLE VERSE

'… for they themselves report what kind of reception you gave us. They tell how you turned to God from idols to serve the living and true God'
(1 Thes. 1:9).

REFLECTION

The believers in Thessalonica turned to God from idols, the one true and living God who will not tolerate rivals. When visiting a country like Nepal, where Hinduism is the majority religion, it is difficult to comprehend people recognising and worshipping 33 million gods. Idols and images are everywhere, and the devotion displayed at the various shrines is heartbreaking. Idolatry in any form is an attack on the character of God Himself and reveals the spiritual blindness of the perpetrator. The gospel exposes the futility of worshipping either gods of silver and gold or unknown gods. Two hundred and seventy-five people groups in Nepal remain unreached by this message. That's over 25 million people who still need to hear of the one true and living God who has made Himself known in Christ.

PRAYER

Lord, I come to You today acknowledging that You are the one true and living God. Thank You for the reassurance of knowing that You are able to hear my prayer and answer. I pray for the millions of Hindus in Nepal who will bow before idols today, vainly hoping that their prayers will be heard. Please bless the witness of Your people in Nepal and cause the light of Your Word to shine into the darkness. I ask that many more in that land will hear the good news, reject idols and turn to You.

DAY 61

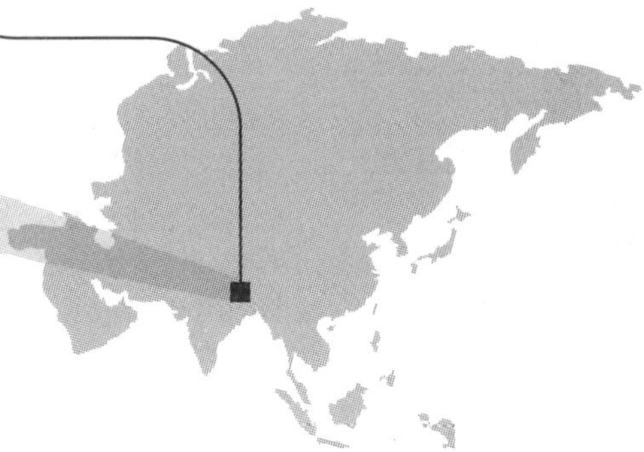

NEPAL

Part 2

It takes a while to escape the city, but you eventually reach the countryside, only to discover that the roads are lethal! Your driver regularly points out locations where buses have gone over the edge, doing little to calm your nerves. The journey to the Saptari district in south-eastern Nepal is long and tiring so you long for a good night's rest afterwards, but sharing your room in the guesthouse are dozens of geckos. You know they can't do you any harm and are actually very good at keeping mosquitoes away, but their presence unnerves you nonetheless.

At 5 a.m. you awaken as the call to prayer sounds out from loudspeakers in the mosque across the road. Although predominantly Hindu, there is a sizable Muslim community here too.

Later, you create a stir as the jeep drives into a remote village and stops outside a small group of dwellings. Soon, you're climbing a narrow bamboo ladder and crawling into a small loft where the church meets. This is the least evangelised region of Nepal, and home to the Tharu people group who number over two million. Eleven others join you for worship and you are invited to share a few words, which need to be translated first from English to Nepali, then to Tharu. At the time of your visit, John's Gospel has only recently been translated into the Tharu language and is the only Scripture available in these people's heart language. Sitting among this small group of believers, you feel so far removed from them in culture and language, but in a strange and wonderful way they feel like family. That sense only grows as you share a delicious lunch of dal bhat with massive portions of rice.

BIBLE VERSE

'... faith comes from hearing the message, and the message is heard through the word about Christ' (Rom. 10:17).

REFLECTION

The Great Commission tasks us with making disciples of all nations, but since faith comes from hearing the Word of Christ, we must awaken ourselves to the truth that discipleship is impossible without the Bible. Many of us would be amazed if we were to count the number of Bibles in our homes. On top of that, there are thousands of commentaries, devotional books and study materials available to us in the English language – which we so often take for granted. However, of over 7000 languages spoken in the world, only around ten per cent have a full Bible. Quite a few others have the New Testament or other portions of Scripture translated, but there remain almost 4000 languages without a single verse of Scripture. Today, a small team of translators continues the painstaking work of producing a Bible in the Tharu language.

PRAYER

Lord, thank You for my Bible. Please forgive me when I take it for granted or fail to read it as I should. I pray for teams translating the Bible into Tharu and other minority languages. Give them wisdom, insight, accuracy and endurance as they labour for You in this task. Lord, continue to build Your church among the Tharu people. As more portions of Scripture become available to them, please help them to keep growing in their faith, and hasten the day that every tribe, tongue, people and nation can read the Bible in their heart language!

DAY 62

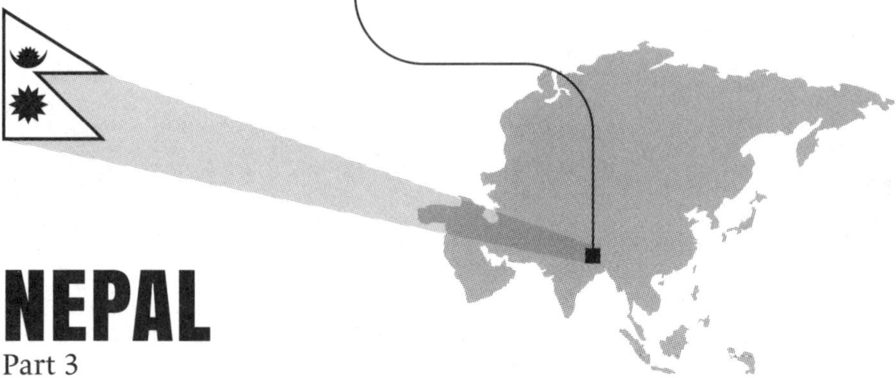

NEPAL

Part 3

You meet Gandira, a Nepali evangelist, who has taken a three-day drive in his jeep from Kathmandu, followed by a 12-hour hike. Thankfully, it's the dry season and, although some of the river crossings were a bit hairy, no diversions were required. He wouldn't dream of attempting the journey during monsoon season. He is here with a group including a nurse, a schoolteacher and two pastors. His plans include a medical clinic, eye tests, the distribution of blankets and mosquito nets, several gospel presentations and three days of Bible training for the region's pastors and church planters. You are all warmly welcomed on entering the village.

Just before you fall asleep, a puzzling thought occurs to you. This is probably the most remote place you've ever been, and they're expecting around 30 pastors and evangelists at this training session tomorrow! Throughout the following morning, as people start arriving from across the region, you discover some have hiked for several days from distant villages and remote communities throughout the mountains. These pastors and evangelists are sharing the gospel and planting churches in some of the most inaccessible parts of the world – one might even say 'the ends of the earth'. Although you can't understand the language, you get a strong sense that they are a real band of brothers and sisters. You feel challenged as you hear their stories, learning of the great hardship and persecution they face in their labour of love. These pop-up teaching seminars are the only opportunity they have to gather and be taught and encouraged in the Scriptures – a stark reminder of how under-resourced the church in Asia can be.

BIBLE VERSE

'Therefore, my dear brothers and sisters, stand firm. Let nothing move you. Always give yourselves fully to the work of the Lord, because you know that your labour in the Lord is not in vain' (1 Cor. 15:58).

REFLECTION

Paul encouraged the Corinthian believers that their trials and hardships were worth it. He was well qualified to write this, having endured many trials in his service for the Lord. It became illegal to evangelise in Nepal when the government introduced anti-conversion laws in 2017. Although officials are unlikely to enforce this law in remote areas, it is not uncommon for Hindu radicals to take the law into their own hands – many pastors and evangelists have been attacked or had their homes destroyed. Training conferences are organised in remote parts of Nepal for pastors and evangelists who would otherwise have no opportunity for Bible training. Gospel tracts and other evangelistic literature are also made available. The workers take as many as they dare, knowing that they become targets for persecution if caught with these materials and yet longing to abound in the work of the Lord.

PRAYER

Lord, thank You that nowhere is beyond Your reach and that even in inaccessible mountain villages You are building Your church. Please bless the labours of pastors and evangelists in Nepal, helping them as they share the gospel. I pray that as people read tracts and other literature, You would open their eyes and draw them to Yourself. Please protect and strengthen Your people in the face of persecution. May the church in Nepal be steadfast, immovable, always abounding in Your work, knowing that their labour is not in vain.

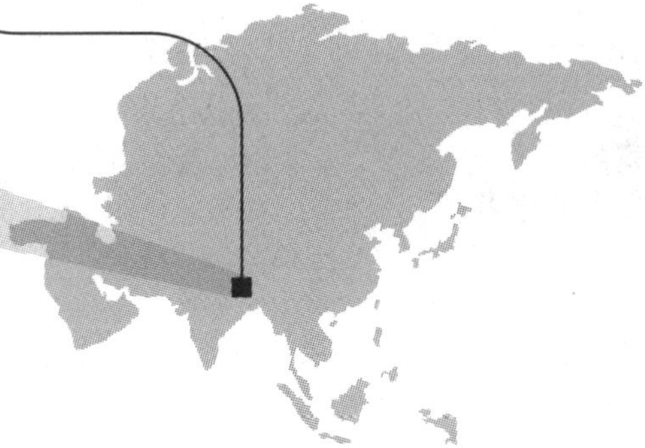

NEPAL

Part 4

You are back in Kathmandu for one final day in Nepal. With so much still to see, you hire a little taxi for the day to zigzag across the city and visit various sights. Your first stop is the Monkey Temple, a holy site for both Buddhists and Hindus where monkeys wander freely and try to steal your snacks. Your taxi driver insists that you photograph his car number plate before heading in. You realise this was a good idea when you descend the temple steps later to find innumerable identical taxis lined up!

The traffic is chaotic travelling to the Pashupatinath Temple on the banks of the Bagmati River. As you traverse the large temple grounds, you are glad you paid the few extra rupees for the guided tour. Hindu holy men with painted faces pass by and pose for photographs.

The memory of the final part of the tour will never leave you. Standing on a little footbridge looking downstream, you count ten square platforms on the edge of the river. Smoke and flames rise from several of them as temple attendants poke and prod at the fires. Some seem to have been recently lit while others have almost burned through, now reduced to a pile of smouldering ash. Meanwhile, grieving family members stand nearby, watching as the bodies of their loved ones are cremated. The remains are pushed off the plinth, unceremoniously and without dignity, into the dirty, stagnant water below. This hopelessness weighs heavily on you. Did those lost souls ever have the opportunity to hear of Christ, our living hope?

BIBLE VERSE

'Praise be to the God and Father of our Lord Jesus Christ! In his great mercy he has given us new birth into a living hope through the resurrection of Jesus Christ from the dead' (1 Pet. 1:3).

REFLECTION

The core message of the gospel is that Christ not only died for our sins but was raised from the dead. Through the resurrection of Jesus, we have a living hope. Standing at the Bagmati River with such a graphic picture of death being played out before your eyes, the contrast between Christianity and Hinduism could not be more stark. Hindus long to die near such cremation sites in order to have their ashes scattered into one of the holy rivers, all in an attempt to appease the gods and obtain a favourable reincarnation. The Hindu idea of climbing the ladder in this life to secure a better lot next time around typifies works-based religion but offers no sure hope – after all, who knows whether they've been good enough? Yet the gospel offers the certain hope of new life through faith in Christ's death and resurrection.

PRAYER

Lord Jesus, thank You for dying on the cross so that I can have forgiveness of sins and a living hope in You. I am thankful and humbled that I live in a part of the world where the gospel has been proclaimed for generations. Please deepen my burden for unreached people across the world and for the lost in my neighbourhood. In response to all You have done for me, Lord, I lay my life before You. Please help me to discover Your plans for my life and use me to bring this living hope to others.

DAY 64

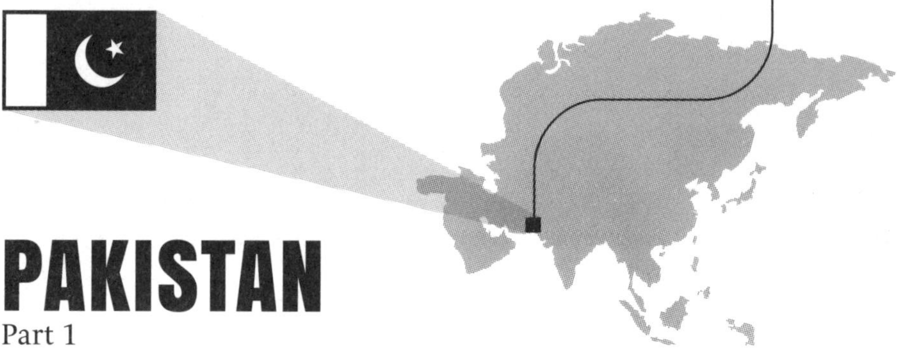

PAKISTAN

Part 1

Once part of Imperial India, Pakistan is a modern nuclear power. Its population of over 212 million is predominantly Muslim, with Christian and Hindu minorities comprising just 3%. You present your documents nervously to the immigration officer, hoping that all is well with your visa and passport. You survey his light-blue shirt with navy-blue epaulettes before, to your surprise, he waves you through disinterestedly. On the other side of the inspection booth, you almost bump into one member of a family throng greeting a returning relative. Rose petals are thrown on him and a few of them land on you.

You are collected by Latif and two others, before finding the traffic chaotic to your eyes. Rickshaws weave between lanes, overtaking bullock carts of wheat while narrowly avoiding pedestrians and overladen trucks. Eventually, you arrive at a Christian school to find an oasis of quiet order. The children rise to greet you as you enter the first classroom. They are clearly excited to have a Western visitor and some giggle shyly.

Michael tells you he is glad to be studying here. When he went to an ordinary school, he was bullied for being a Christian. He couldn't eat or drink with the other students, and few of the teachers supported him. He shows you his textbooks with evident pride, particularly in his maths work. He is now catching up on his studies after falling behind. Next, you meet a girl who is receiving an education for the first time in her life, despite already being 12 years old. Thanks to this school, she has access to the learning her parents could not afford. They work as bonded labourers in nearby fields, but with their daughter attending school, the family can finally look forward to a better future.

BIBLE VERSE

'Whoever welcomes one of these little children in my name welcomes me'
(Mark 9:37).

REFLECTION

The Scriptures reveal the heart of the Father and His special affection for children. The Lord Jesus famously invited children to Him, and bids us to welcome and receive children in His name. He sets us an example to imitate. Indeed, our acceptance of children is a sign of our receiving Christ Himself. So many children in Pakistan have parents who cannot afford to pay school fees, and many Christian children find school life intolerable due to the discrimination they routinely face. Yet education is essential in breaking the cycle of poverty and empowering the next generation; a good school gives protection to children and can bring about generational change. These children are so keen to learn. All they need is the opportunity.

PRAYER

Lord, thank You that I have had so many opportunities to learn in various contexts, for those who have taught me and for the privilege of a good education. I ask that You would meet the need for children in Pakistan, especially those from Christian homes, to receive a life-transforming education. I pray that Muslim children and families would come to know the Saviour as they hear the gospel at Christian schools. Please protect these schools, the teachers and the children from opposition. Lord, please make these places springs of life-giving water in the desert.

DAY 65

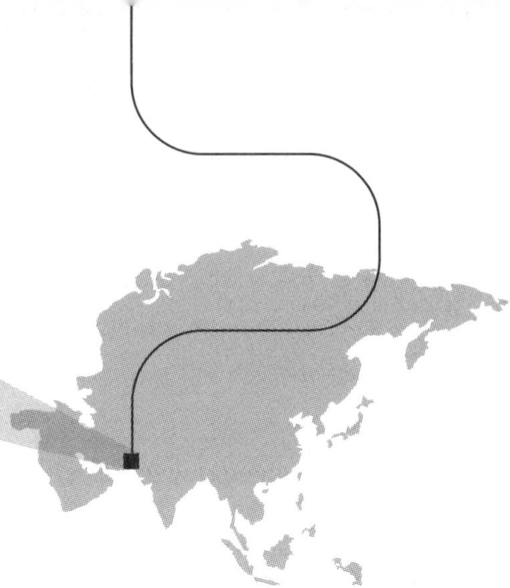

PAKISTAN

Part 2

Today, you travel with Latif to a brick factory. It is nearing 30°C in the late morning, so you are relieved the vehicle has air conditioning. Despite seeing pictures online, nothing has quite prepared you for the reality as a 100-foot-high, soot-blackened stack comes into view. Smoke oozes from the top, grey-black against the blue sky – a giant cigar pointing to the sun. Around 20,000 brick factories operate in Pakistan, employing ten million people. Despite child labour laws, two million of these workers are minors. Workers must produce 1000 bricks each day. By adding water to the clay soil, they make a paste and press each wad into a mould, much like a shallow baking tin, before tipping bricks out in rows of hundreds. The pay can be as little as £1 per day.

Latif explains that the bricks will be placed in the wood-fired kiln, whose emissions are severely detrimental to the workers' health. Even worse, these families, often illiterate, are at risk of becoming indebted labourers. Many end up borrowing money for medicines, funerals or other necessities at high rates of interest, with loans becoming a means of control as repayments are taken out of already meagre wages. Although this loan system was outlawed in 1992, it remains widespread. Debts are rarely repaid, often being passed down through generations. Those who complain about long working days or poor conditions may be beaten, women can be sexually abused and appeals to the law will rarely be considered.

'This is why we are providing a school for these children,' Latif continues. 'They can learn to read and write. They can learn their rights and make a better future for themselves – one of hope, where we break the cycle of poverty, debt and bondage.'

BIBLE VERSE

'He has sent me to bind up the broken-hearted, to proclaim freedom for the captives'
(Is. 61:1).

REFLECTION

The prophet Isaiah paints a picture of the glory of Zion and the blessings to come for God's people. At the start of chapter 61, the blessings turn from economic prosperity to freedom and healing. Broken hearts will be bound up (v. 1), mourners will be comforted (v. 2) and captives will be liberated (v. 1). Those working in the brick factories of Pakistan face the same longings for freedom as God's people in Isaiah's day. They are paupers in need of financial rescue. They are heartbroken people in need of healing. They are captives in need of liberation. But many do not know the Lord's compassion and justice. They do not know His comforting promises. They do not know His salvation.

PRAYER

Heavenly Father, how great is Your compassion on the sinful, the poor, the broken-hearted and the captive. Thank You for the mercy You have shown in saving me from my sins, and for the grace I receive each day through blessings I do not deserve. Please bring an end to the illegal and exploitative practices taking place in Pakistan, and act justly against the oppressors. May the bonded labourers who know You be comforted by Your promises, and may Your Word reach others so that they too might find hope and salvation in You.

DAY 66

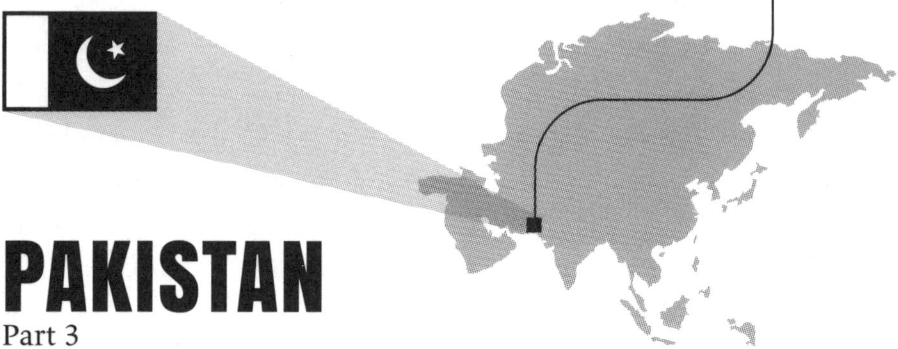

PAKISTAN

Part 3

You step along the side street, trying to avoid the puddles, while your guide, Atfat, leads the way. Hearing upbeat singing and percussion, you wonder if it comes from the church you are headed for in this poor quarter of town. As you turn down another alley, the brick facade of the church appears, though it has no cross. You step over the threshold of a shuttered entrance into a small courtyard. The congregation is in full view, sitting on the ground, women to the left and men to the right. A small child eyes you quizzically before nestling her face in her mother's lap. A woman leads the singing with hands raised and waving, her eyes closed as she praises the Lord with joy. Next to her, a man plays a tabla to keep the rhythm. The congregation clap their hands to join in the celebration.

The church in Pakistan is under pressure. Christian converts have typically come from Hinduism's lower castes and routinely find employment opportunities restricted to the most menial jobs. Conversion from Islam, while not illegal, is fraught with difficulties. Estrangement from family, beatings, false legal proceedings and even death can be the price for turning to Christ. Yet still there are those who do so. Though life as a Christian is tough, with careers and educational opportunities curtailed, the hope of eternal life is counted more precious. Christians in Pakistan know the true value of the pearl of great price.

You join in the praises, clapping your hands and praying for the church to be protected from evil, strong in faith and bold in witness. Above all, you are thankful for what you are learning from these humble, joyful brothers and sisters.

BIBLE VERSE

'Again, the kingdom of heaven is like a merchant looking for fine pearls. When he found one of great value, he went away and sold everything he had and bought it'
(Mt. 13:45–46).

REFLECTION

The Christian faith is an exchange. It is a deal, a trade, a cost-benefit analysis. Perhaps you've not considered it that way before, or think this manner of speaking is unworthy of such sacred things. But Jesus draws a comparison in this parable: the cost of following Him is represented by the merchant selling all he had. Imagine deciding to buy an object which would cost everything else you had. After the trade, you would have this and nothing else. Would it be truly worth it? Christians who face suffering, particularly persecution, must ask themselves, 'Is the kingdom worth it? Is Jesus worth it?' Those believers suffering for their faith in Pakistan answer with a resounding 'Yes!' He is worth it.

PRAYER

Lord, I believe that Your Son is the Messiah and truly worthy of adoration. Please help your church to bear gladly the burden of following the suffering Saviour. Help me to count the cost, to believe that it is a price worth paying, and to see that having Jesus means having everything. Please enable me to despise the ridicule of the world and the hardships of discrimination, should they come. Make me seek Your approval only. Please protect, bless and extend Your kingdom in Pakistan, so that Your praises may resound in Punjabi, Pashto, Sindhi, Saraiki and Urdu!

DAY 67

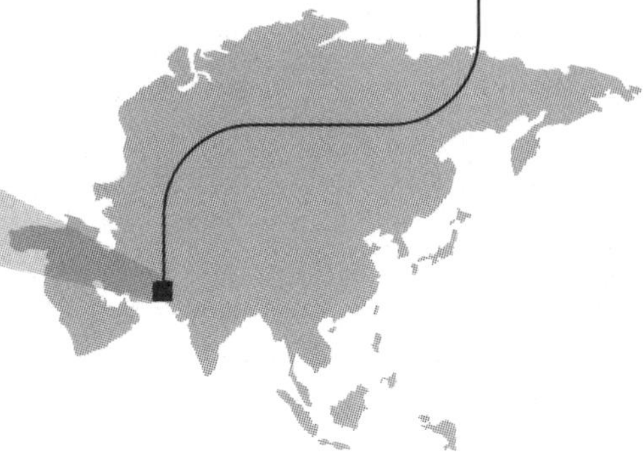

PAKISTAN

Part 4

On your first morning in the rural south, you wake up in a small village. The sun is tentatively peering over the horizon, poised to blaze over all you see. Hearing a goat bleat behind a high-plastered wall, you go to investigate. A girl and a young man are putting goats and cows to pasture, fastening them by ropes in a communal grazing area. Nearby, an older lady in a pink sari pumps cool water into an aluminium container. In the centre of the village, a group of women and children squat around the low, earthen stove as black-grey smoke rises lazily above them. A young girl tends the fire while her mother adds dough to the flat, black pan.

A group of 15 men arrived last night. Latif explains that they are training to be evangelists and each month come together to learn a story from Scripture – this time they are learning about the Good Samaritan. They will memorise the story and recount the details to each other before discussing what it means and how to apply it to the people they will meet. They do not take Bibles with them since their audiences are poor and illiterate. Instead, they witness by telling the story, and then establish a church around those who respond to the message. Each of these 15 workers will visit many villages in the next month, explaining the story of the Good Samaritan to many thousands and sharing the gospel with all who will hear. Next month, they will come back here to share what happened and to pray for one another. Then they will learn another story, go back out to the villages and continue to repeat the cycle.

BIBLE VERSE

'How beautiful on the mountains are the feet of those who bring good news' (Is. 52:7).

REFLECTION

How joyful we are when we receive good news; we are even pleased with the one who delivers it! So connected are the messenger and the message that we remind each other not to shoot the messenger if they bring bad news! Those who bear the good news of salvation are highly esteemed in God's sight; even their feet are beautiful. They declare peace between man and God, and the happiness that comes from His reign in the human soul. Sadly, the world does not always esteem these heralds of the gospel. Christ's servants publish peace, but are sometimes treated as delegates of discord. However, where they and their report are received, there is joy. Evangelists in Pakistan walk a fine line, seeking to win the lost in the face of real opposition. They need the wisdom of serpents and the innocence of doves (Mt. 10:16).

PRAYER

Lord, please protect and encourage Your evangelists in Pakistan. I pray that their labours would bear much fruit and that Your Spirit would work powerfully in that nation. Please let the numbers of evangelists grow, and raise up pastors for new churches. Open the hearts of all who hear the gospel to receive the message of peace, and grant wisdom to Your servants as they seek to win the lost. Please give them boldness in their message and joy in knowing You. Lord, You reign, but I pray that Your reign would be acknowledged much more widely in Pakistan.

DAY 68

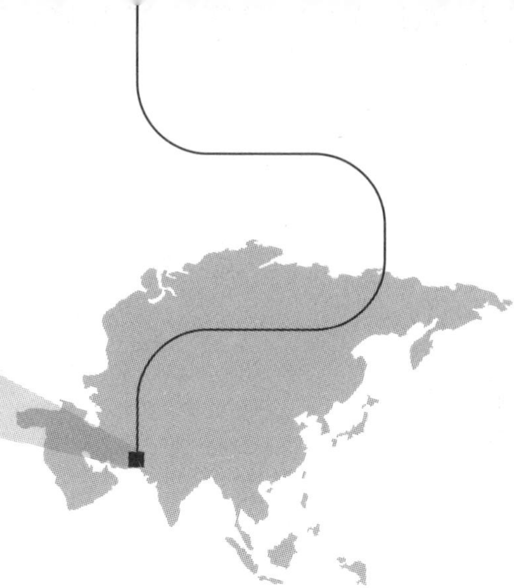

PAKISTAN

Part 5

You enter through a brown, steel gate into a concrete courtyard. To your right is a cream, plastered brick wall; in front is a small, square window and a door which leads into the building. This is a home for underprivileged children, established by Latif and his organisation. It is lunchtime, and as you enter the dining room, a boy of about ten years, in a light-blue shalwar kameez, stands up to pray, fervently giving thanks for the curry and roti bread on everybody's plates. After he sits down, a girl in a red sari stands up to add her thanks. Multiple spoons then scrape joyfully on tin while you meet the team and learn more about the home. The cook sets down some extra side dishes, having emerged from the small kitchen adjoining this communal area. Another man is responsible for cleaning and general upkeep. Next, you meet Bushra, who teaches the children English and leads some of the regular devotional times. Each child has their own copy of Scripture to read regularly.

You begin to see that as well as providing food, shelter and safety for the children, the home meets their spiritual needs too. It is a holistic provision. The children stay because they come from remote villages with no schools. Here, they can access Christian education at an excellent school down the road, and have their learning supplemented back on site. You visit one of the dormitories, which features six wooden bunk beds and an en-suite bathroom and shower, but the children urge you to follow them out to the yard. Two boys are particularly eager to impress you with their acrobatics, competitively cartwheeling in a whirl of brown and grey kameez. Sheer joy marks their faces!

BIBLE VERSE

'*... faith by itself, if it is not accompanied by action, is dead*' (Jas. 2:17).

REFLECTION

True faith, James explains, goes beyond mere words. It is a faith which acts. It sees need and is moved to meet that need. True religion is not the mere profession of faith or the recital of a creed. If a child has no access to education, then true faith works to teach that child. If a child is hungry, the religion that God accepts puts bread on the table (1:27). If a child is thirsty, a Christian is to give water. Of course, it is an essential part of our faith to seek the eternal good of the spiritually hungry and thirsty, but our calling also involves the here and now – the things needed for the body (2:16). This children's home is a gleaming embodiment of both the physical and spiritual elements of our calling as faithful followers of Christ.

PRAYER

Lord, help me to profess Your name in deeds as well as words. Please strengthen all Your people in Pakistan who are working to meet the needs of others. I pray that children would find access to education and a secure place to live, and that those living with them would always have hearts full of mercy and compassion. Thank You that You care for orphans and the least in society. Please provide for, protect and bless the children at this home, and allow similar homes to be opened to meet the needs of other children in Pakistan.

DAY 69

INDIA
Part 1

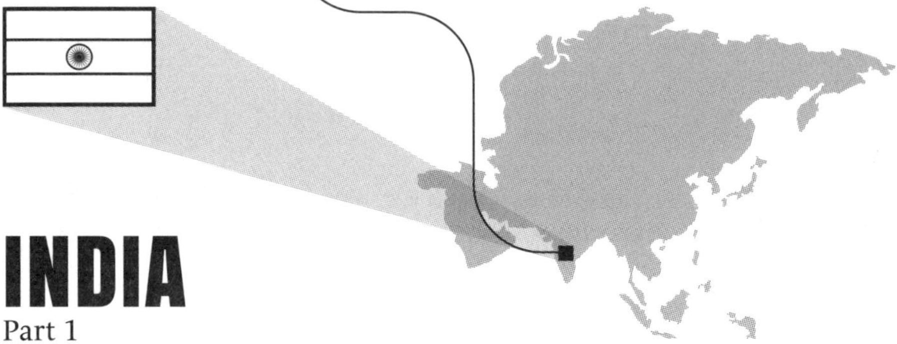

With Indian and Pakistani nationals unable to cross the border, just a handful of European businessmen take the daily flight from Lahore to Delhi. Your onward connection then takes you to Srinagar, the largest city in Jammu and Kashmir.

This region has suffered violence between India and Pakistan for decades, with both nations claiming authority here. The power struggle is evident even upon landing, with the airport resembling a military base. You pass numerous mosques and several military checkpoints on the drive into town before asking why so many broken bridges remain unrepaired. Your host, Jamal, explains that terrorism has discouraged the authorities from investing in infrastructure, fearing it will simply be destroyed once again. The instability has also scared tourists away, causing unemployment to rocket. As you enjoy the beautiful vistas of Dal Lake and reach the quaint houseboat upon which you will stay, you are saddened that this beauty is so overshadowed by darkness.

Jamal takes you to a fellowship of believers who are small in number but mighty in spirit. They meet in secret, changing the time and location of their gatherings to avoid detection. Hannah owns a salon through which she engages local women in gospel conversations. She also runs sewing classes for women in the villages, teaching them truths about Jesus through songs as they work. Karim had been like many secret atheists here – someone who had lost faith in Islam but was afraid to tell his friends and family. After trusting in Christ through an online debate, his goal is to befriend and share the truth with other atheists, praying that they too might finding joy and salvation in Christ.

BIBLE VERSE

I have told you these things so that in me you may have peace. In this world you will have trouble. But take heart! I have overcome the world'
(John 16:33).

REFLECTION

To meet with believers in the underground church is a powerful and sobering experience. You see first-hand the impact of their marginalisation, preventing the regular and public fellowship to which most of us are accustomed. And yet we should not be surprised. Even Jesus was marginalised and considered crazy by His own family (Mark 3:21), while His opponents sought to kill Him long before His eventual death on the cross (John 8:59). In this world, God's people will have trouble, but take heart! Jesus has overcome the world. There is nothing that can separate us from God and nothing that can take away our salvation! And so, like Hannah, Karim and countless others, let us take up our cross daily, proclaiming the gospel, sharing in Christ's suffering and awaiting His glorious return, confident of our reward in heaven.

PRAYER

Heavenly Father, thank You so much for the good news of the gospel. I pray that You would give me a fresh hope in that radical message, today and every day. Thank You for the hidden gatherings of believers which take place not only in Kashmir but in every place where Your people are marginalised and persecuted for their faith in You. Please give these brothers and sisters confidence in Your faithfulness, justice and power. Help them cling to Jesus through every trial and boldly speak of Him as they await their reward in heaven.

DAY 70

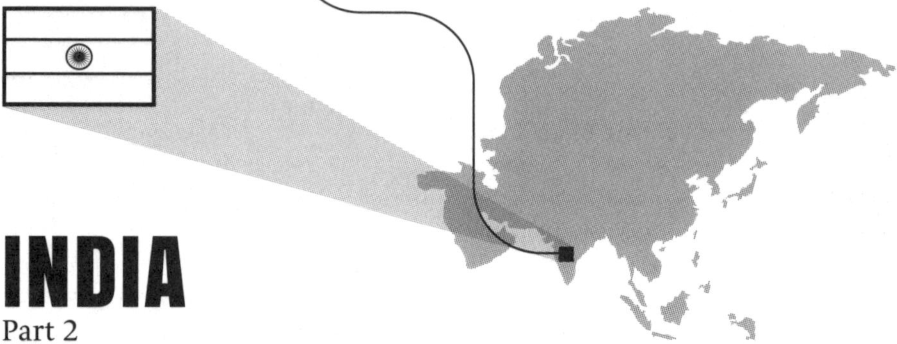

INDIA

Part 2

Back in Delhi, you visit the city centre and take in the colonial architecture of India Gate and Connaught Place. You are relieved to shelter from the hot sun in an air-conditioned coffee shop while you wait for Vijay, a local worker. After you take a seat, though, a young man asks if he can join you and you motion to him to sit. He introduces himself as Tej. He is from Nepal but is studying here in Delhi. Stories are shared before he offers some advice for navigating the capital. 'You helped me with this seat, so I will help you,' he says. His conditional approach to grace jars with you as Jesus' words spring to mind: 'Even sinners love those who love them … But love your enemies' (Luke 6:32, 35).

After Tej departs, Vijay arrives and takes you into Central Park. There, his team have gathered dozens of young people into an active community who share songs, food and life together. With so many people coming from all over India (and beyond) to study here, many lack any sense of belonging. Vijay and his team seek to provide that.

Vijay introduces you to Yuvaan, who he then urges to share his testimony. 'I study music and some classmates brought me here two years ago,' he says. 'I arrived here looking for new experiences, new friends, a new community. I enjoyed getting to know people, playing music for them and listening to others, but the best part has been the talks by Vijay and the team. They are always interesting and I was fascinated by the teachings of Jesus. Eventually, it all fell into place and I understood God's grace. I guess the Holy Spirit was working in my heart all along!'

BIBLE VERSE

'You are bringing some strange ideas to our ears, and we would like to know what they mean' (Acts 17:20).

REFLECTION

Paul would go from one city to another engaging large gatherings of people with the gospel. First, he and Barnabas set out from Antioch (Acts 13:1–3) to preach in Cyprus, Pisidian Antioch, Iconium, Lystra and Derbe. By Acts 16, Paul was embarking on another journey with a new team alongside him. They shared the gospel in Philippi, Thessalonica and Berea before arriving in Athens, where the local philosophers were intrigued by the new teaching they were hearing. It is hard to imagine hearing of Jesus for the first time. Most of us have always had some notion of who He is, even if only through the nativity story. For those who have never heard, the gospel is strange, new information, and many are eager to learn more! Praise God for those workers in Delhi, for Yuvaan's testimony and for many other changed lives in that city!

PRAYER

Father God, thank You that You designed us to live in community, and for the blessings experienced when Your people gather together in fellowship. Thank You for my church family, and for all the believers who have impacted my life, including those who shared the gospel with me for the first time. Thank You for Your grace to me! Please use the team in Delhi to bring that grace to others, so that many more lost souls might find their way into Your kingdom.

DAY 71

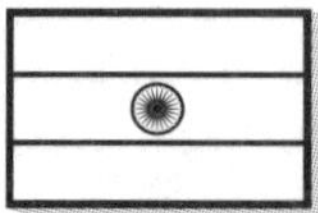

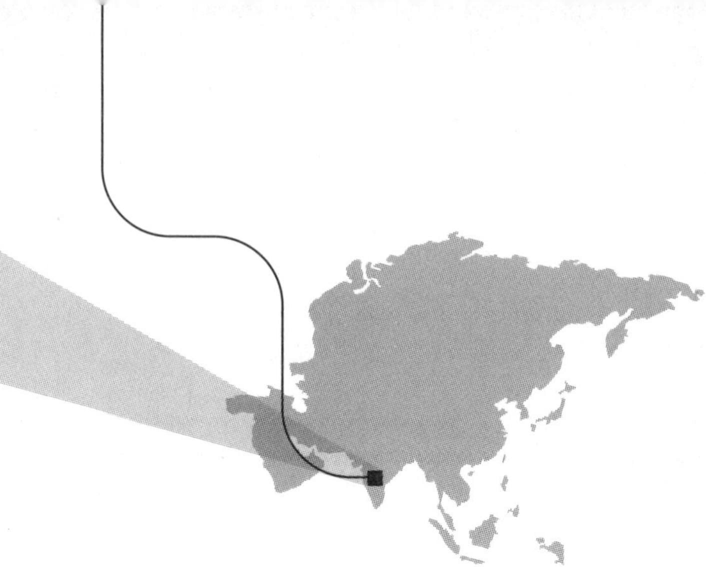

INDIA

Part 3

Five hundred miles south-east of Delhi lies the bustling city of Varanasi. The streets are a hive of activity as Hindus flock to the banks of the deified River Ganges. They believe that she rescues those who die here from the painful cycle of reincarnation and the struggles of this world.

Families are taking recently passed loved ones down to the funeral pyres at the water's edge. Death hangs heavy in the air and your heart aches to witness hundreds of people resting their eternal hope on the dirty waters of this ancient river. But when Darshan, whom you are meeting, begins to explain his work, you are relieved that gospel witness exists amid this all-consuming darkness. Nearby lies an ashram set up by Darshan and his team – a space for the community to escape the darkness of this living, breathing funeral parlour. The site houses a church and school, and provides opportunities for local people to learn vocational skills. Most significantly, the ashram is a place where the news of salvation in Christ is shared with all who will hear.

Darshan says the children's summer programme has been a particular highlight. Hundreds of youngsters made crafts, played games and heard the wonderful news of Jesus Christ. Christmas was another busy time, with over 1000 people joining a celebration at which food was served and the gospel proclaimed. Dozens of baptisms have been taking place each year and hundreds now join together for Bible studies. However, the vision goes far beyond this community. The long-term goal is to establish centres in ten further districts in the area. It is a remarkable ambition, but we have a remarkable God.

BIBLE VERSE

'... you have made the heavens and the earth by your great power and outstretched arm. Nothing is too hard for you' (Jer. 32:17).

REFLECTION

God told Jeremiah that the city of Jerusalem would be captured by the Babylonians. King Zedekiah did not take kindly to the message, and did not trust the Lord's Word, so imprisoned Jeremiah in the temple courtyard (vv. 2–3). Jeremiah's faith was also tested. The Lord told him to buy a field – a strange thing to do when the land is about to be captured by your enemies and will soon become a desolate waste without people or animals (v. 43)! Nevertheless, Jeremiah had faith in God's plan and bought the field (v. 9) because the Lord had said, 'houses, fields and vineyards will again be bought in this land' (v. 15). From an earthly perspective, this seemed impossible, but Jeremiah trusted in the mighty power of God. Praise God that Darshan and his team are showing the same kind of faith with their great vision for Varanasi!

PRAYER

Lord, You are more mighty and powerful than I could ever understand or imagine. You made the heavens and earth by Your great power. You appoint kings and rulers, and are sovereign over the nations. Please help me trust in Your power and plans! I thank You for the work taking place amid the darkness of Varanasi. Please use Your people to bring truth and life to a city cloaked in death. Lord, bless the vision for many centres to be established, so that all may hear the good news of eternal life in Christ.

DAY 72

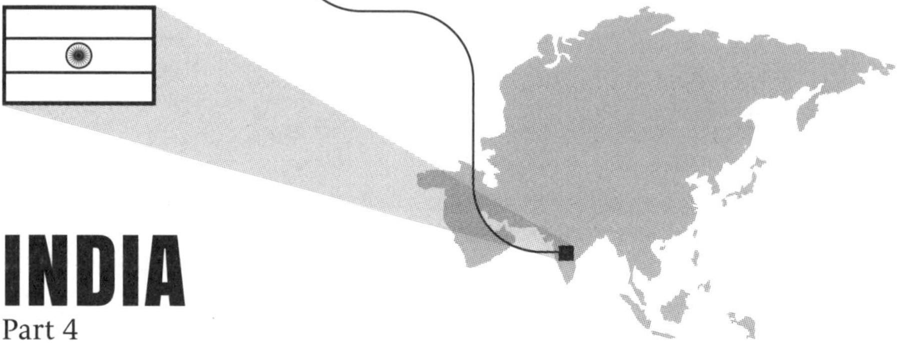

INDIA

Part 4

It can be hard to grasp how vast this nation is. After travelling south from Delhi, you find yourself in the little-known city of Vijayawada. Despite the three-hour flight, you remain 1,000 kilometres north of India's southernmost point. In a small village outside the city, you soon encounter the region's poverty. Villagers live a hand-to-mouth existence, fully reliant on the small patches of land they own to grow food and provide an income. A quarter of India's population lives on less than 35p per day and some dare not dream of earning more.

Your spirits are lifted, however, as Vikram, your host, explains the ministry here. Vikram supports a network of small churches in the local villages. The people you meet have had the opportunity to hear the gospel and join a church. When you visit a service, you marvel at the vibrant congregation. They passionately love and serve the Lord. To help alleviate the financial burdens here, Vikram practically supports the elderly and those unable to work by providing a monthly pension. Your heart breaks as you meet some of the recipients and pray with them, asking the Lord to reveal Himself to them and bring them blessing.

Finally, you visit a children's home on the outskirts of the village. Before entering, you hear excited voices and the pitter-patter of little feet running inside. Here, dozens of orphans are offered a safe home which is full of love. The baggage carried by some is harrowing, yet now they have broad smiles on their faces, enjoying the education on offer. Above all, this is a place where Christ is made known and these children love hearing about the great God who created them.

BIBLE VERSE

'Whoever oppresses the poor shows contempt for their Maker, but whoever is kind to the needy honours God' (Prov. 14:31).

REFLECTION

For many of us, money is not in short supply, making it difficult to comprehend the difficulties faced in villages like this. Families must survive on next to nothing, the elderly are left destitute if they have no family to care for them, and many children find themselves without homes through no fault of their own. Truly, rural India is home to some of the neediest people on our planet. At least in the cities there are opportunities for work. In the countryside, there is only what you can make off the land. It is a joyful thing to hear of people like Vikram who work to combat such poverty. The elderly are cared for, children are lovingly raised and the gospel is proclaimed widely in word and deed. Whoever is kind to the needy honours God. What opportunities do you have to put this into practice?

PRAYER

Lord, thank You that You care for the needy in our world. Thank You that even though our world might overlook or neglect people like those in rural India, You never do. Please give me a heart for the poor and help me to honour You by showing kindness towards them. Thank you for Vikram and for all You are doing through him. I pray that through his network of churches and ministry, many would be freed from spiritual poverty as they discover the abundant riches of faith in Jesus Christ.

DAY 73

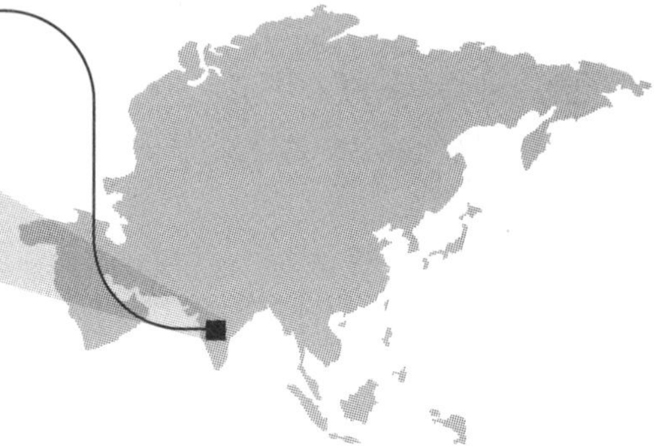

INDIA

Part 5

In the tropical, southern state of Kerala, the scene before you is a complete contrast to the hustle and bustle you experienced in the north. The streets are lined with palm trees, fishing boats lie in rows along golden beaches, and birdsong forms the acoustic backdrop. The way of life here is slower, more relaxed, more peaceful. Around half of Kerala's population are Hindus, with Muslims making up one-quarter and Christians roughly one-fifth. There is relative freedom for believers here – you even notice Bible verses painted onto walls around the city in both English and the local Malayalam language with its distinctive, curly Brahmic script.

Around 20 million tourists visit Kerala each year. Most come from other parts of India, but a healthy number also arrive from Europe. Hotspots include Trivandrum, Kochi, the exotic tea plantations of Munnar and numerous houseboat routes along lazy backwater rivers. It is a beautiful place.

After sampling the area's natural beauty, you return to Trivandrum to meet Jassar at his small shop in the city's backstreets. There he repairs electronic equipment, but his passion is not for technology. Instead, he uses the shop as a platform for engaging with expatriates from the Maldives, many of whom come here to study. Jassar has found that fixing broken goods gives him great opportunities to befriend his customers, share life stories and explain the reason for his hope in Christ. Being a staunchly Muslim people group, it is not easy to win converts for Christ among the Maldivians. However, this is an incredible opportunity considering the restrictions Jassar would face reaching these people in their own nation.

BIBLE VERSE

'Live such good lives among the pagans that, though they accuse you of doing wrong, they may see your good deeds and glorify God on the day he visits us'
(1 Pet. 2:12).

REFLECTION

The gospel message is unchanging, but the methods used in cross-cultural mission vary from one time and one place to another. The classic view is of Western missionaries being sent out to preach good news to the lost, but God's workers in the harvest field today use many different strategies. Jassar's approach is nothing new! Peter urged his readers to live among the 'pagans' day by day, conducting themselves in a godly manner and bringing glory to God, even amid opposition. Whether through fixing electrical goods, running tour companies or establishing cafes among unreached groups, many modern missionaries seek to live good, 'normal' lives among the unreached groups around them, befriending them and pointing them to Christ in both word and deed. There is room in mission for the evangelist, the vet, the hairdresser, the mechanic and more! Which of your God-given gifts could be used in cross-cultural mission?

PRAYER

Heavenly Father, thank You that You guide my steps and that Your Word is a light unto my path. I pray that You would help me to recognise and develop the gifts You have given me. Please help me to see opportunities to use them for Your kingdom, whether at home or abroad. Please also bless Jassar in his daily labours for You. Give him many opportunities to show Your love and speak of Your grace, particularly among the Maldivian community in his city.

DAY 74

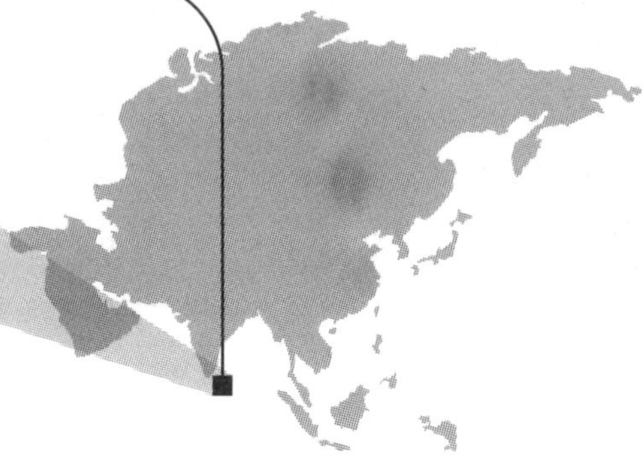

SRI LANKA

Part 1

You have so far visited many unusual and unfamiliar parts of the continent, each opening your eyes to new practices and ways of life. You have been used to a heightened sense of anticipation while walking the streets of other countries. But here in Colombo, the capital city of this island nation, that feeling is replaced with a comfortable sense of familiarity. The scene is not altogether dissimilar to some European cities. The sun is gloriously bright, but the proximity to the sea means there is little humidity. The streets are wide, with clean pavements from which tall palm trees grow. These are lined by the storefronts of boutiques and idyllic cafes, with tourists noticeable throughout much of the city. Even the traffic is less busy than in most Asian destinations, and is certainly the calmest you have seen on your travels. You have never felt safer zipping about a city in a rickshaw!

It is incredible to think that a peaceful place like this was embroiled in civil war as recently as 2009. Tensions remain, but the most recent act of violence suffered here was religiously rather than politically motivated. On Easter Sunday in 2019, 269 people were killed as bombs were detonated at various locations including three churches. An Islamic extremist group claimed responsibility.

However, the Lord is still working here. You meet a local Christian who tells you that the bombings opened up some incredible gospel opportunities. Many people wondered why Christians didn't retaliate after the attacks, and believers were able to explain the essence of the gospel to those enquiring – that Christ forgives all those who have sinned against Him if they repent and put their faith in Him. Freely forgiven, the Sri Lankan believers have been able to forgive others in turn.

BIBLE VERSE

'And forgive us our debts, as we also have forgiven our debtors' (Mt. 6:12).

REFLECTION

At the heart of the gospel is a message of forgiveness and reconciliation. All have sinned against God; no one outside of Christ can be counted as righteous. Each one of us needs the forgiveness which was bought at the cross, and is offered freely through God's gracious gift of faith in Him. As we examine our hearts, the extent to which we need this forgiveness becomes clear. Despite this, forgiving others still doesn't always come naturally to us, even in the little things! What a witness Sri Lankan Christians are as they forgive those who attacked their brothers and sisters. Others can only look on them in wonder. Praise God, who even in the worst of situations is able to bring about good for His glory!

PRAYER

Lord, I owe everything to You and to Your Son, Jesus. Thank You for the cross and for the forgiveness which has been offered to me. Please help me to forgive others as You have forgiven me. Thank You for the ways in which You have used the witness of Your servants in Sri Lanka. Only You can bring good from the darkest situations. Please continue to use believers there as a light for the gospel, bringing glory to Your name as Your Spirit works in the hearts of Your people.

DAY 75

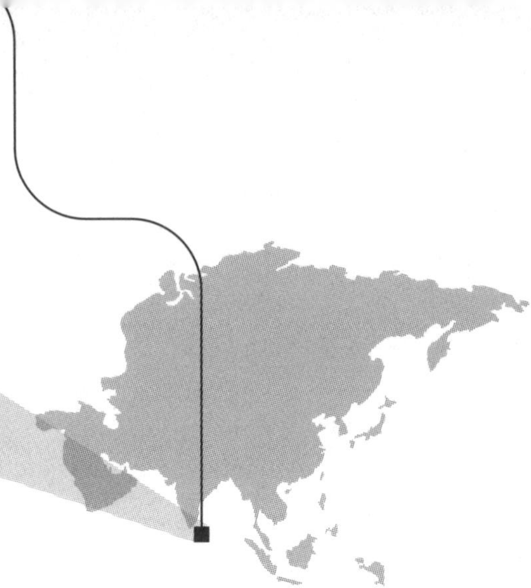

SRI LANKA

Part 2

As you wander the streets of Colombo, you stumble across multiple temples full of tourists and worshippers alike. These are temples dedicated to the worship of Buddha. The air is filled with the smell of burning incense and you hear the low, serene chanting of various Buddhist mantras. Around the temple are elaborate statues depicting gods and demons alike, while before the statue of Buddha in the centre of the temple lie offerings of food and money. Over 70% of Sri Lankans are Buddhist, believing that Buddha sees all they do and judges their actions. Good and bad actions are thought to have causal effects on one's future, with consequences played out in this life and lives to come. Do good, and you might be reincarnated wealthy and prosperous. Do bad, and you could be born as an animal or plant. The majority of people in Sri Lanka will live and die believing this to be truth.

Praise God, then, for the group of believers you meet today. They run a ministry focused on God's Word and are passionate about enabling many to hear the gospel. Regular outreaches are held, through which the claims of the Bible are faithfully taught and explained. These brothers and sisters in Christ also operate a powerful youth ministry, with as many as 145 young people gathering at their events to discuss Christian perspectives on big issues. Leaders from local churches also benefit by receiving training in how to tackle these issues biblically in their home congregations. Discipleship and ministry training are key priorities for this group. Men and women are being trained in the gospel so that they in turn can play their part in the advancement of God's kingdom. Praise God for raising up these servants for His work!

BIBLE VERSE

'Don't let anyone look down on you because you are young, but set an example for the believers in speech, in conduct, in love, in faith and in purity'
(1 Tim. 4:12).

REFLECTION

Timothy was a young man in a position of big responsibility. Left behind by Paul to minister to the Ephesian church, he had a lot on his plate. With the Lord's help, he stepped up and set the believers he was shepherding an example. It was a difficult task, especially when we remember the sinful culture Timothy found himself in – one full of false doctrine (1:3–7), blasphemy (1:20) and immodesty (2:9). It is thrilling to hear that so many young people in Sri Lanka are hungry for God's Word. Our prayer for those receiving this excellent Bible teaching, as well as those leading them, is that they will set an example in their godliness too.

PRAYER

Lord, thank You for Your Word which speaks truth even today, and for those proclaiming the good news in Sri Lanka. While the world is ever-changing, You and the truths of Your Word are not – they remain the same yesterday, today and forever. Thank You for planting Your Word deep in the lives of young people in Sri Lanka. May they grow into mighty men and women of God, persevering in godly living and doctrine that many might be saved through their witness.

DAY 76

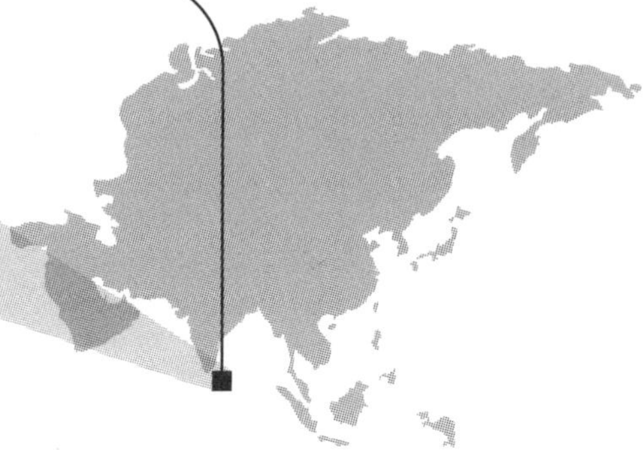

SRI LANKA

Part 3

You have one final day to spend with these eager believers who are earnestly seeking to advance God's kingdom in Sri Lanka. So many have a real burden for this Buddhist-majority nation. While they remain very much in the minority, the church here has been richly blessed with solid Bible teaching through which the Lord has built them up and added to their number.

As you speak with these brothers and sisters in Christ, you discover that there is also a deep and passionate yearning to make God's name known beyond the shores of this island nation. Christian leaders here are encouraging believers not only to enter into theological training and reach their own people, but to go out into the wider mission field also. The movement of Sri Lankans being sent abroad for gospel ministry is well underway. You hear of some Sri Lankan missionaries who are reaching people in Bangladesh, while another couple are preparing to begin a new ministry in Myanmar. You are told that investigatory trips are also being made to northern India and other nations in the region. The church here has readily accepted the challenge to go and make disciples of all nations!

These believers are heeding the call of the Great Commission and going out to make Christ's name known wherever He might lead them. How encouraging to see so many believers being mobilised for mission outside of their own nation! May the Lord continue to build His church here, in both depth and breadth, and may He send many more Sri Lankans into the mission field to proclaim the riches of His grace in Christ!

BIBLE VERSE

'Then he said to his disciples, "The harvest is plentiful but the workers are few. Ask the Lord of the harvest, therefore, to send out workers into his harvest field"'
(Mt. 9:37–38).

REFLECTION

The verse above is a real challenge to our thinking. Reading it can often convict us of how irregularly we pray for there to be more workers for the harvest. Hopefully, the stories of Sri Lankans being sent into the mission field will serve as an encouragement to our prayers. The Lord is raising up men and women to serve Him in His world, even in those places like Sri Lanka which rarely cross our minds as 'sending nations'. What a thrill to know that the Sri Lankan church has caught the vision of our global God! Let's keep praying earnestly, as we are instructed in verse 38, that there would be more workers for the harvest. Let us also listen to the Lord to discern whether we might become an answer to that prayer ourselves.

PRAYER

Lord, thank You for the church in Sri Lanka and for those mobilising Your followers for mission. I praise You for each and every Sri Lankan who has entered the mission field and pray for Your help and blessing upon them and their ministry. There remain so many in this world who do not know or acknowledge Your name, and who do not know the saving power of the cross. I pray that there would be more workers for this harvest, and that You would lead me to serve You wherever and however You desire.

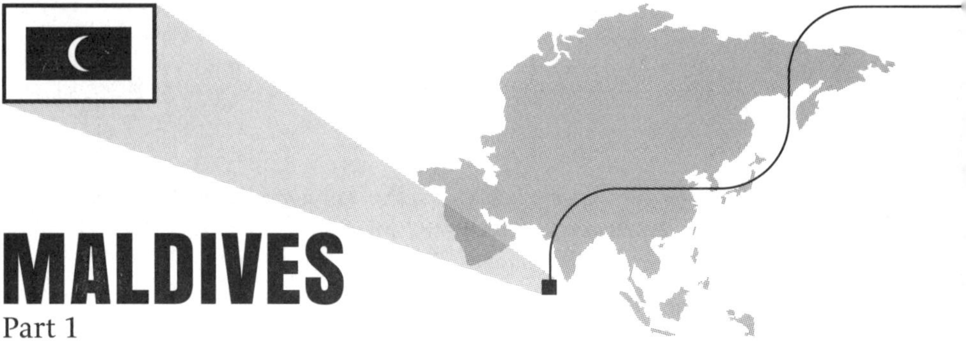

MALDIVES

Part 1

Where the sky meets the ocean along the far-off horizon, you see the subtle difference in shades between the two. From the plane window, there is little else to see, with the deep blue ocean unspoiled by land or ship beneath the cloudless sky. The plane turns in the air. From nowhere, specks appear in the water below. Coral reefs encircle large groups of tiny islands resting in shallow, turquoise waters. In the middle of the Indian Ocean, hundreds of miles from any other civilisation, lie the Maldive Islands. One of the most remote nations on earth, it is usually visited only by honeymooners and the super-wealthy. With many of the 1000-plus islands uninhabited, the government has been known to sell them off for the right price. As the plane descends, you can see the attraction. White sandy beaches, palm trees, crystal clear waters and glorious weather make this something of a paradise on earth.

The main international airport is found on an artificial, floating island, so you hop straight onto a boat with your luggage before setting sail for the nearby capital, Male. On arrival, you discover a very different side of the Maldives. This city is not an idyllic holiday resort – it is a poor man's Manhattan in the middle of the Indian Ocean. From edge to edge, the island is full of high-rise buildings, narrow streets and countless mosques. This is the real Maldives – a place which is home to just under 400,000 people, with 99.99% of them Muslims. The Maldives are one of the most unreached places in the world today, and life here is far from a paradise on earth. Indeed, these islands are a paradise lost.

BIBLE VERSE

'Jesus answered him, "Truly I tell you, today you will be with me in paradise"'
(Luke 23:43).

REFLECTION

Very few nations are as unreached by the gospel as the Maldives. When we think of the islands, we imagine the picture-perfect scene of sun, sea and sand, with hammocks and overwater wooden huts. We rarely consider their lack of churches or Christian witness. Over the years, very little headway has been made in reaching these islands, yet there are believers here. Living in secret, even amid such beautiful surroundings, they will only know true paradise when they are with Jesus in glory. Do not be deceived by the alluring appearance of the Maldives. Like the man on the cross next to Jesus, the people of these islands desperately need to realise the weight of their sin and come to Christ for salvation. This is the only way to be accepted by the Father, and the only way to enjoy the true paradise of His presence.

PRAYER

Lord, thank You for the gift of Your Son, who died on the cross for sinners like me. Thank You that in Him I have the hope of an eternity spent in a real paradise with You. Lord, I pray for the Maldives. Help me to look past the outward image of these islands to the need of the people living there. Lord, please help me be persistent in my prayers for this remote and regularly forgotten nation. I pray that You would reveal Yourself to the Maldivian people, and that many would come to a saving faith in Jesus.

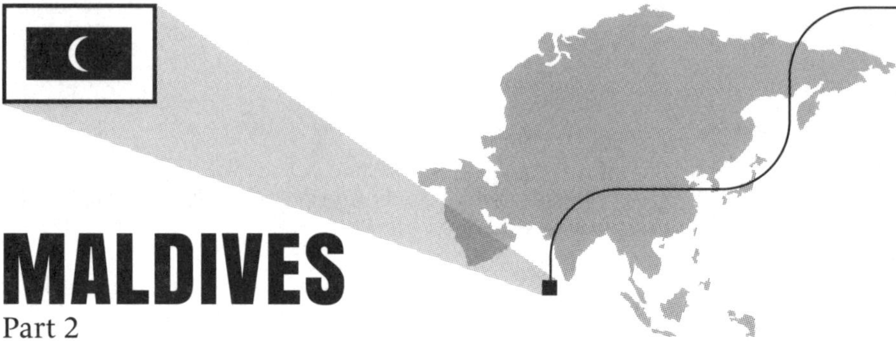

MALDIVES

Part 2

As you explore the city of Male, you come across a shop which catches your eye. Distracted by the seemingly endless waves of motorbikes buzzing by, you almost missed it entirely, but you venture inside and are instantly taken aback by a variety of wonderful scents. The shop is a perfumery. A man behind a counter is mixing ingredients, creating new concoctions. You examine the different perfumes, working out the exchange rate in your head as you go. Eventually, when you've settled on one to purchase, you catch the eye of the shopkeeper and smile expectantly. As he packages up your purchase, you begin to chat. His name is Mohammed. He has been married for 20 years and has three children. His mother is still living. The whole family visit their local mosque together on a regular basis – they are all Muslim. Everybody else you have spoken to has similar stories.

Earlier in the day, you took a boat journey to a small island nearby. There, you met an elderly lady named Nissa selling fresh fruit from her front door. She has lived on that small island her whole life. She too is a Muslim, as are her mother, her grandmother, her great-grandmother and so on. Generation after generation, Nissa's family have lived on the island, attended the mosque and followed the teachings of Islam. Neither Mohammed nor Nissa have ever heard the gospel. There's every chance that you were the first Christian to even speak to them. For hundreds of years, just like the vast majority of the Maldivian people, these families have not had contact with the gospel nor a church nearby through which they might hear it. This is what it means to be an unreached people.

BIBLE VERSE

'Jesus answered, "I am the way and the truth and the life. No one comes to the Father except through me"' (John 14:6).

REFLECTION

The Republic of Maldives prides itself on being the most Islamic country in the world. Entire islands of people will live and die without knowing that the opportunity for salvation is found in Christ … unless the Lord intervenes in miraculous ways. We must burden ourselves to pray for the Maldives – for islands with no Christians and no Bibles, and for a nation with no public church. There is no true hope for these people in Islam; Jesus is the only way to salvation. There is no other truth and no other path to everlasting life. The Maldivian people may not realise it, but they are a people in desperate need of the gospel.

PRAYER

Lord, thank You for saving me. Thank You for revealing the truth about Your Son through the Bible and through those who explained it to me. Thank You that Jesus made a way for me to come to You, my heavenly Father, for forgiveness and eternal life. Lord, please open the eyes of the Maldivian people to the reality of their position before You. Help them to see that there is only one way to salvation and eternal life with You, and that it is found not in Islam, but in the truth of Jesus Christ alone.

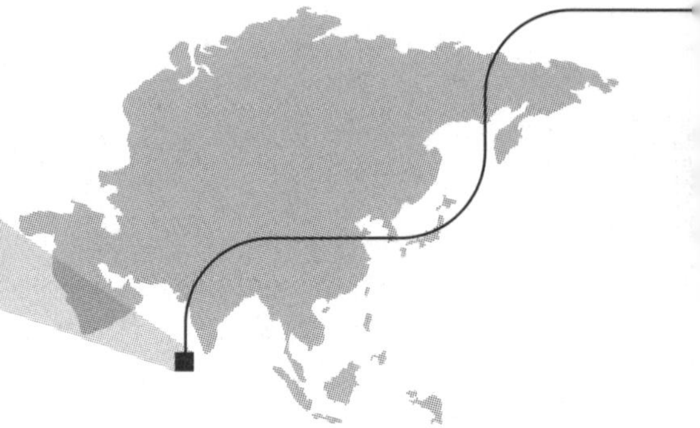

MALDIVES

Part 3

The extent of Islam's grip on the Maldives has been clear, even in these few short days. Back on arrival, the airport had signs warning against the possession of any religious materials contrary to Islam. You were grateful that you had left your Bible at home in favour of an app on your phone. The national flag proclaims the Muslim identity of the islands, depicting the crescent moon. Mosques are found on each of the inhabited islands, yet churches are absent. You wonder how these islands will ever be reached with the gospel, but remember stories of those who have felt called to this place. Individuals visit from elsewhere to support through prayer and fellowship those few Christians who live in secrecy. For some Maldivian believers, this is the only fellowship they have, making it a source of vital encouragement. One local is in a particularly precarious position. Having previously been imprisoned for his faith, he is desperate to see his daughter come to the Lord. However, she is married to a police officer. Time with a fellow believer in prayer for this situation is a great blessing to him.

Another couple trained for years before moving here as missionaries. They started a business through which they got to know many people. Eventually, after a couple of years, they felt confident in sharing the gospel with one local. Shortly after, word got out that they were Christians. Threats were made against the family and they had 48 hours to flee the islands. After so many years of anticipation, the family left with no apparent fruit from their efforts. You leave these islands longing that workers would not be discouraged from coming here to share the gospel.

BIBLE VERSE

'How, then, can they call on the one they have not believed in? And how can they believe in the one of whom they have not heard?'
(Rom. 10:14).

REFLECTION

The Maldives is one of the most difficult nations on earth in which to share the gospel. Many attempts to reach the islands have failed and it is very difficult to bring in Christian materials. The resources available to the Maldivian people are also limited, with this being the only country in the world without a complete translation of Scripture in its main language. Only certain sections of the Bible are available. Those who minister on the islands must do so with great caution. We are privileged to live in nations with a rich gospel heritage, as opposed to these many islands which have barely had contact with the gospel in hundreds of years. Past failures aside, we must continue to pray that the Lord would somehow, some day, establish His church in the Maldives.

PRAYER

Lord, thank You for the access I have to Scripture in my own language. Thank You for enabling me to come alive to it when I heard it, bringing me to a saving faith in Jesus. Lord, I pray that You would open doors where it seems none exist. May those seeking to reach the Maldives be led by the Spirit to find the best way forward. Thank You for their desire to share the good news on these islands. I pray that many Maldivian people would come to know You personally as their Lord and Saviour.

DAY 80

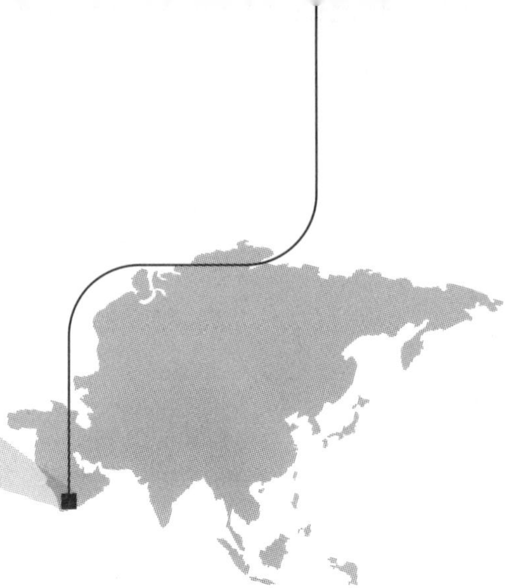

YEMEN

Part 1

As you reach the most perilous point of your journey, you are acutely aware that, as a westerner in Yemen, you run the risk of being kidnapped for ransom. So you seek to be discreet in every action. You have not travelled far into Sana'a, the capital city, when you see the effects of the war which has been raging for years – the bomb damage is only too obvious. You hear that the situation is much worse in some rural areas, where protection from the onslaught is minimal. The fear on people's faces is tangible and the children seem to be the worst affected. This, coupled with the fact that two-thirds of the population do not have enough food, brings home the reality that Yemen represents one of the greatest humanitarian crises on the planet. Famine is real here, not because of crop failures or poorly managed farming, but because of civil war.

Moving around the country, the results of conflict are everywhere and impossible to miss: homes destroyed by seemingly indiscriminate bombing; market places empty because of the lack of food and of people, with many having been killed; and fields laid waste, with bomb craters where food was once grown.

You reflect on this horrible, seemingly hopeless situation, filled with sadness. Only one person and one message could ever bring hope to a place like this, and yet this is a country where Islam is the state religion. Sharia law is embedded in the legal system and, through persecution, the nation forcibly rejects the message of hope in Jesus Christ. And so you pray. You pray discreetly and silently, but you pray, knowing that God hears your prayer.

BIBLE VERSE

'How the cattle moan! The herds mill about because they have no pasture; even the flocks of sheep are suffering' (Joel 1:18).

REFLECTION

The lust for power always leads to the suffering of others. Whether that lust takes place in the political arena, in families or in churches, there are always those who pay the price. The common phrase used these days for the innocents caught up in the struggle is 'collateral damage'. How much collateral damage have we ourselves experienced and how much might we have caused as we have sought, perhaps, to further our own agendas? The way of the cross is the way of humility, calling us to embrace suffering and self-sacrifice for the good of others. Jesus had no agenda other than the will of His Father. He imposed nothing on anyone, and if we are those who seek to follow Him, then neither will we.

PRAYER

Loving God, please break my heart as Yours is broken at the suffering of oppressed people and victims of war. Help me to share Your sense of injustice when great pain is caused to so many by lustful people who seek to impose their own will. Lord, please help me to stand alongside the suffering and the broken in word and prayer and deed, and to make a difference as You enable me by Your Holy Spirit.

DAY 81

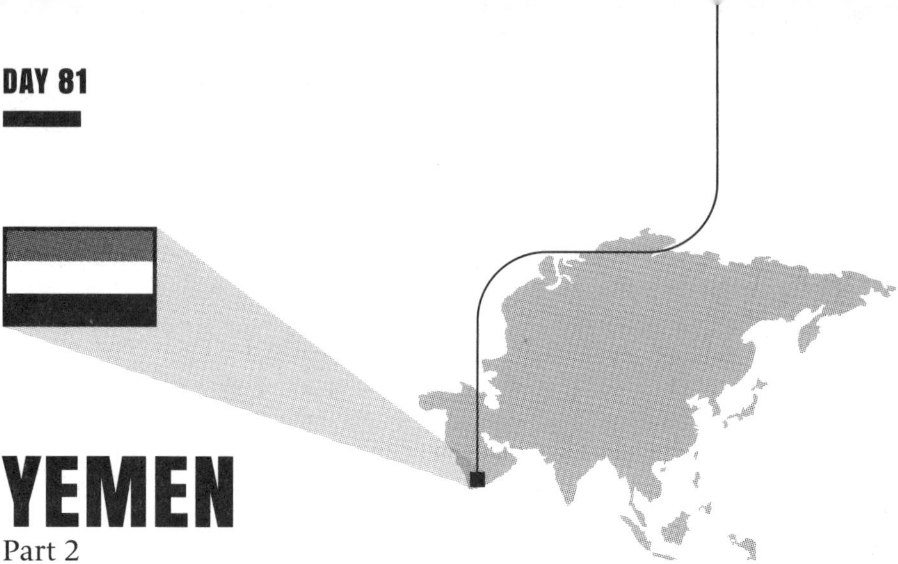

YEMEN

Part 2

You travel to meet Hassan, one of perhaps only 3000 Christians in a country with a population of nearly 30 million – over 99% are Muslims. Because the church is vigorously persecuted here, you are aware that you face imprisonment and Hassan faces the possibility of execution if you are caught.

So you meet in the shadows, then listen to Hassan's story of coming to faith in Jesus through reading the Bible. He comes from a Muslim family who as yet know nothing of his conversion. In this, he tells you, he is not alone. He wants to be baptised as a follower of Jesus and you marvel at his courage and devotion. He is truly willing to risk all for Christ. You ask if he knows of any other Christians and he says, with a face filled with sadness, that he does not. You ask how he is able to grow in his faith without fellowship and he replies that the Holy Spirit is his fellowship. You wonder if you would be able to maintain a faithful walk in similar circumstances.

Later, you meet with a Christian foreign aid worker whose identity and nationality are not disclosed. He tells you that despite the existence of church buildings in the southern city of Aden, many have been destroyed in the war and others have been closed by the authorities. You comment on the sadness of this but he remains upbeat because the church, the faithful following of Jesus, is growing among Yemenis. Despite the persecution and the fact that every Yemeni is deemed to be a Muslim and forbidden by law to leave Islam, the truth of Jesus is being made known and embraced. You share a smile and quietly give thanks for this incredible truth.

BIBLE VERSE

'Blessed are those who are persecuted because of righteousness, for theirs is the kingdom of heaven' (Mt. 5:10).

REFLECTION

One of the greatest freedoms that we have, and one which our society probably takes for granted, is the freedom to believe what we want. Imagine living in a country where what you believe is imposed on every citizen. Imagine being part of a society where you have come to believe that Jesus Christ is the only hope – not just for you but for your whole nation – but you are not free to speak of Him, or of His love and grace and mercy. You are not free to speak of His life, death and resurrection. You are not free to worship with others who also acknowledge Jesus as their Lord. Living openly for Jesus is not always as simple and easy as we might think.

PRAYER

Thank You that the Lord Jesus came to seek and to save those who are lost. Thank You for His death on the cross, paying the price for my sin and opening up the way for me, and all who will come, to be forgiven. Lord, I pray for those who know and love Jesus but are denied the right to live openly for Him. Please grant them Your grace and strength, and give them a deep and inexpressible joy even in the midst of their persecution.

DAY 82

SAUDI ARABIA
Part 1

You arrive in Riyadh acutely aware of how few westerners have, historically, been allowed to explore this corner of the world. With so much history behind the region and this being one of the wealthiest cities in the Middle East, your mind buzzes in excited anticipation. You decide against using the metro, opting to travel above ground instead. Palm trees line the road, punctuating your view of seemingly infinite desert, before you enter the business district and eventually reach the heart of the city. Here, street vendors sell freshly prepared shawarma while innumerable food outlets offer kabsa, baklava, nuts and more. Fried chicken, pizza, sushi and burritos are also readily available, while shopping malls house Western retail chains alongside local brands; you even spot an IKEA.

The scorching heat of the day makes evening the time to explore. You enjoy an ice cream and admire the dancing fountains of the well-lit King Abdullah Park, alongside families who have emerged from the mosque and now sit together on blankets. While Muslim women in Southeast Asia wear colourful attire, black abayas are the norm here, worn with a burqa or hijab. Men wear traditional thawbs, sometimes beneath a suit jacket. Dress codes are a point of tension, particularly since rules were relaxed to attract tourists. Occasionally, you notice a local wearing modest Western attire.

Four per cent of the population are considered Christian, but this figure is almost exclusively migrants from the US, Europe, Korea, China, Indonesia and the Philippines. Over 90% of Saudis are considered unreached by the gospel, with apostasy punishable by death. This law is rarely utilised, but 100–200 people are executed each year for crimes including murder, drug offences, rape and adultery, making the law a strong incentive to reject the gospel.

BIBLE VERSE

'For it is by grace you have been saved, through faith – and this is not from yourselves, it is the gift of God – not by works, so that no one can boast'
(Eph. 2:8–9).

REFLECTION

Walking around Riyadh, you will see people attending the mosque for prayer, dressing a certain way and avoiding certain foods. During Ramadan, visitors will notice people fasting. Later in the year, tourists will encounter some of the millions making the pilgrimage to Mecca. These rules and rituals are followed out of an earnest desire to obey the will of Allah, to be righteous and obtain his favour. However, favour with the true God cannot be earned. He made us alive with Christ when we were dead in transgressions (v. 5), richly showering us in grace and mercy rather than judging us on our imperfect performance. We are saved by grace, through the gift of faith which has been given to us (v. 8). Saudis have begun to accept outside influences in food and even in fashion, but the message of faith in Christ continues to be rejected.

PRAYER

Heavenly Father, thank You that, in Your rich mercy, You made me alive with Christ, even when I was dead in transgressions. Thank You for graciously giving me the gift of faith and not treating me as my sins deserve. I pray for Saudi Arabia. Please loosen the stronghold which Islamic faith has on the nation, allowing gospel seeds to grow and the church to blossom among these people.

DAY 83

SAUDI ARABIA
Part 2

You head out, eager to study the nation's history. The Masmak Fortress is a significant structure, strongly resembling a giant sandcastle, with displays of antique guns and historic costumes. The storming of the gate here in 1902 began 30 years of events, culminating in much of the Arabian Peninsula being united as the Kingdom of Saudi Arabia. At the National Museum, the history of Islam is the primary focus.

What visitors to these sites do not discover is the biblical history played out within the nation's borders. Much of the Exodus narrative took place on the Arabian Peninsula. First, Moses fled from Egypt to Midian – now the north-western region of Saudi Arabia. An ancient well is rumoured to be where he met his wife, Zipporah, and tours now take place to sites such as 'Jethro's caves in the land of Midian'. The events which unfold from Exodus 15 onwards (after the crossing of the Red Sea) all took place here, with some believing that Saudi Arabia's Jebel al-Lawz mountain (the 'almond mountain') is the historic Mount Sinai where the Ten Commandments were given.

However accurate these supposed locations may be, this region clearly played a significant role in biblical history. The Quran itself teaches that God revealed the Torah (Genesis to Deuteronomy), the Zabur (psalms) and the Injil (gospel) to Moses, David and Jesus respectively. Nevertheless, many Muslims never study these books, largely because of accusations that the texts have been corrupted over time. While these accusations can comfortably be dismissed by historical evidence, they continue to discourage Muslims in Saudi Arabia and around the world from examining the truth of the biblical Scriptures for themselves.

BIBLE VERSE

'All Scripture is God-breathed and is useful for teaching, rebuking, correcting and training in righteousness, so that the servant of God may be thoroughly equipped for every good work' (2 Tim. 3:16–17).

REFLECTION

How sad it is that the people of the Arabian Peninsula are so unaware of the incredible acts of God in and around their homeland. Having rescued His people from Egypt, God led them across the Red Sea and into modern-day Saudi Arabia, with Moses as their leader. The Lord gave His people the Ten Commandments and the rest of the Law, guiding them into a right relationship with Him, all the while providing atonement for their sin. We are privileged to read the Old Testament, meeting Him there and seeing the countless signposts to Jesus' eventual arrival. Meanwhile, Muslims are discouraged from doing so through false accusations that these Scriptures have been altered and added to over time. Tragically, so many are seeking truth, and a right relationship with God, yet are looking in all the wrong places.

PRAYER

Lord, thank You for the mighty works You performed in rescuing Your people from slavery in Egypt. Heavenly Father, thank You for rescuing me in Christ from bondage to sin and into the freedom of a loving relationship with You. Please burden my heart for the lost. Give me such a love and compassion that I pray earnestly for them, and long to support efforts to reach them. Please help many Muslims discover that the Bible is true and is Your Word to a lost world so that they too can find rescue in Christ.

DAY 84

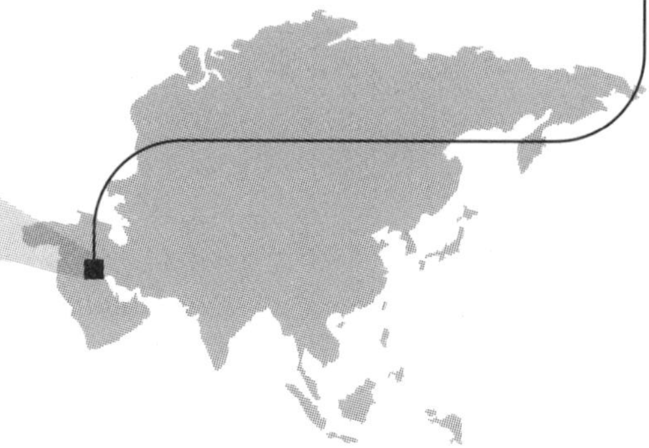

IRAQ

Part 1

You arrive at the airport in Erbil only to find that those due to greet you are not permitted to enter the terminal building. You follow the crowd onto a bus and eventually find Hassan and Faisal, who embrace you warmly. Welcome to Kurdistan! Over the coming days, you will be exploring this northern corner of Iraq with these friendly hosts.

Driving to your hotel, you are struck first by the noise and extent of the traffic, then by how Western the city feels. Very few women wear veils, with most opting for Western clothing, while almost no men wear anything resembling your understanding of Middle Eastern dress.

In speaking with your hosts, you realise just how much Kurdistan and Iraq feature in Old Testament history. Heading north-west to Zakho, you pause at a bridge over the Kebar River – the river where Ezekiel saw visions of God. As you stand on the bridge watching youngsters swimming below, you imagine standing beside Ezekiel as God revealed Himself to the prophet, and feel goosebumps on your flesh. South of Zakho lies the small town of Alqosh – the Elkosh where Nahum lived, ministered and died. His tomb is still there today and you stand before it.

Slightly further south lies the city of Mosul, outside of which are the ruins of Nineveh, the city central to the story of Jonah. Away from Kurdistan, near the city of Basra in the south-east of Iraq, are the ruins of Ur of the Chaldees, the original home of Abraham. The history of the Bible and of God's activity is all around you. Indeed, you realise that this is your history as a follower of Jesus, and you give thanks and worship.

BIBLE VERSE

'The Lord had said to Abram, "Go from your country, your people and your father's household to the land I will show you"' (Gen. 12:1).

REFLECTION

Coming to a place like Kurdistan and visiting some of the places mentioned in the Old Testament can really deepen our awareness of how wonderful God's plan is for a broken and sinful humanity. From Ur, Abraham travelled 700 miles to the borders of present-day Iraq, another 700 miles into Syria, another 800 down to Egypt by the inland road and then back into Canaan – modern-day Israel. Abraham trusted God and obeyed Him, thus unlocking the plan and the promise of God, made in Genesis 12. Right up until this present day, God has not changed, His plan has not changed and the means to unlocking the plan of God in our lives has not changed. We are called to trust Him, to follow Him and to obey Him, just as Abraham was.

PRAYER

Heavenly Father, thank You that You are the unchanging God. You are the God who spoke to and called Abraham. You are also the God who has spoken to and called me, first of all to come to Yourself and then to step into Your will and purposes. When I hear Your voice, may my first response be like that of Abraham: to obey Your call. Help me to listen for Your guiding voice day by day, and to serve You always.

DAY 85

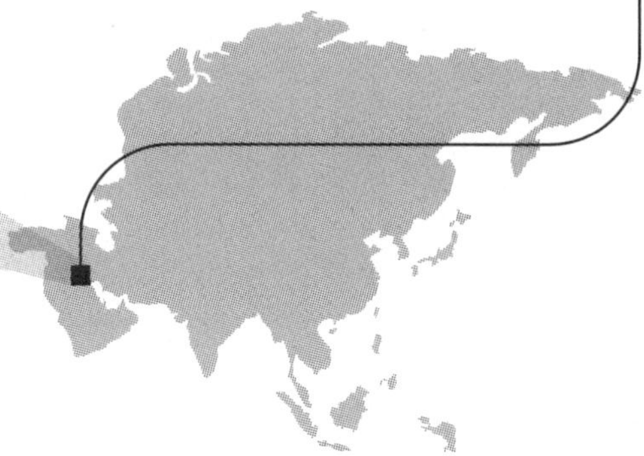

IRAQ

Part 2

You feel a nervous anticipation as you approach a refugee camp, home to 7000 refugees mainly from the Yazidi people group. You are made aware of the need both to be quiet and to blend in, as far as possible. Absolutely no photographs are to be taken of the camp. Entering a small room, you notice that Christian literature covers all of the walls, except one filled by a huge map of the world. Christian books and booklets are placed on a number of desks and seem to form a literary mosaic.

Pastor Aram, who has brought you here and whose church finances the outreach work in this camp, introduces you to Kyaram. He is a Yazidi man who escaped the ISIS assault on Mount Sinjar in 2014 and has lived in the camp ever since. He tells you his story.

'When coming to the camp, I was given a Bible which my father took from me. Thankfully, another person gave me a Bible on a memory card for use in my mobile phone. For the next few weeks, I spent my time reading this Bible, almost from morning until night, and God spoke to me through it. I recognised my sinfulness and my need for Christ to be my Lord and Saviour, and I gave my life to the Lord Jesus Christ.'

You are thrilled to hear this story of God's love and power. But you are truly challenged when Kyaram adds that he is now working as an evangelist, seeking to share the love of God and the message of Christ with others in this camp. So the camp is what he now calls home.

'Will you ever be able to go back to Sinjar?' you ask.

'No, but I am where God wants me and can use me, and that is all I need.'

BIBLE VERSE

'… if you declare with your mouth, "Jesus is Lord," and believe in your heart that God raised him from the dead, you will be saved' (Rom. 10:9).

REFLECTION

Have you ever given someone you don't really know a tract, a Bible or some other piece of Christian literature? Perhaps you wondered if it would do any good, fretting whether they would ever read it. And if they did, how would they respond, and to whom? We can often overcomplicate situations like this. Instead of being willing to just be the messenger, we want also to be the manager. The best thing that we can do is to share the message, pray and let God be God. He is the One who works in people's hearts to draw them to Himself, and when He does, the results are staggering.

PRAYER

Lord God Almighty, You save all those who put their trust in Jesus Christ, Your only begotten Son. Please remind me regularly that my mission is to lovingly and boldly proclaim the good news of Jesus to all with whom I come into contact. Thank You for those who shared that good news with Kyaram, and for his response of faith and service. Please use him to share the gospel with many others in his camp, that they too might truly and sincerely confess Jesus Christ as their Lord.

DAY 86

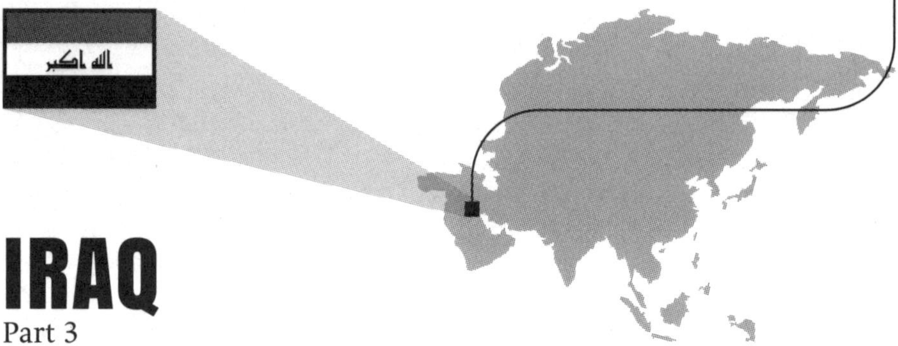

IRAQ

Part 3

Your eye is caught by what looks in the distance like a sea of toilet roll holders, halved sideways, placed on their sides and painted white. The landscape is filled by them. But these are tents, mainly supplied by the United Nations and home to more than 27,000 Yazidi refugees. The tents are basic, with concrete floors which are freezing in winter and boiling hot in summer.

Inside the camp, you enter an English language class for 12 young women, each a survivor of ISIS sex slavery. Like thousands of others, they were taken from their families and traded as brides for ISIS 'soldiers' or kept as slaves to be used and abused. The eldest here is 22 and the youngest only 14. Only now are these women able to tolerate a male presence. For a short while, you are offered the privilege of sharing the love of God in Christ with them. As you leave, you pray that they might find salvation and healing in Him.

Next, you visit a couple with two young children. You eat the food offered, knowing that they may go without as a result, but aware that to refuse would be disrespectful. You listen as they explain how they came to faith in Jesus. The wife first heard the gospel after being invited to a Bible study in the camp, and she longed to learn more. But, being illiterate, she could not read the Bible. Your eyes widen as she explains that instead Jesus appeared to her in a vision and called her to Himself. She did so, followed almost immediately by her husband. You are humbled that despite their harsh surroundings and impoverished lifestyle, this couple want to be used by God to reach their neighbours with the life-changing message of Jesus.

BIBLE VERSE

'Then he said to them all: "Whoever wants to be my disciple must deny themselves and take up their cross daily and follow me"' (Luke 9:23).

REFLECTION

When we read passages that call us to surrender our whole selves to God and to His will and purpose, what goes through our minds? Do we take an inventory of all that we are, and all that we have and hope for? Or do we willingly lay it all before the Lord because our burning desire is to live our lives for His glory? Jesus said that the mark of a disciple is a life of self-denial, where we acknowledge that all that we have and are is a gift of God's rich grace. Is it hard? Yes! But it is right and it is the pathway to experiencing the fullness of life which Jesus promised. Are we true disciples of Christ?

PRAYER

Gracious and loving God, thank You that You gave up Your only begotten Son that He might bear my sin, and the sin of all who trust in Him. Lord Jesus, thank You that You gave up your life to death, paying that great price for my redemption. Holy Spirit, please fill me with a love for Father, Son and Holy Spirit. May that love lead me to give myself wholly to Christ, to truly be His disciple for the glory of Your name.

DAY 87

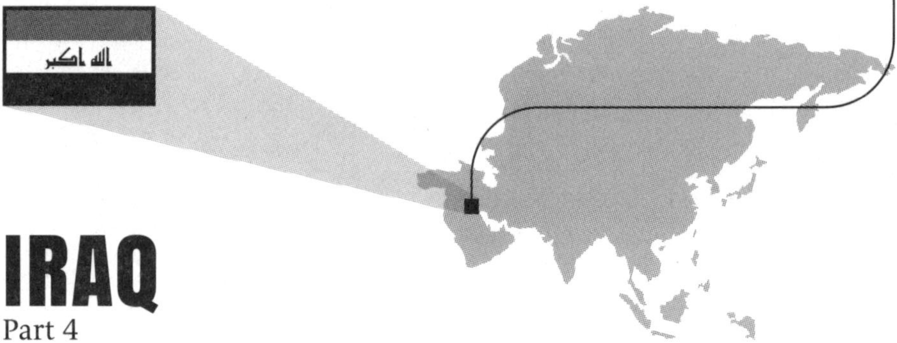

IRAQ

Part 4

You are taken down a backstreet to what looks like a hotel and climb a couple of flights of stairs. At an apartment door you are greeted by a woman, her brother and her teenage daughter. There are younger children asleep in bed, though you wonder where because the apartment is so small. The woman tells you of her escape from Syria after her husband had been murdered by terrorists who planted an improvised explosive device. She had to sell everything she had. Here, she is not allowed to work and her children are not allowed to attend school, but they are safe. She wants to emigrate to Australia to seek a better future for her children. However, her eternal future is secure. Since coming to Iraq, she has been shown the love of Christ by your hosts and has become a Christian.

That evening, you visit other houses and meet people with similar stories – loved ones murdered in Syria by ISIS or other groups; homes and businesses stolen; threats made on lives. You also hear similar testimonies of experiencing the love of God in Christ – souls being saved, hearts being healed and lives being transformed through the grace of God, lived out by His people.

It is Sunday evening, and you are invited to worship with the church who reach out to these refugees. The building is packed. Meeting the pastor and other church staff, you realise why they are making such an impact among the refugees. The love of Christ shines through them! Those whom you have already met arrive and embrace you, and you are enveloped by the love they exude. Your heart delights in the opportunity to worship the Lord in this place.

BIBLE VERSE

'For we are God's handiwork, created in Christ Jesus to do good works, which God prepared in advance for us to do' (Eph. 2:10).

REFLECTION

In the course of our lives as the people of God, we are sometimes brought face to face with desperate people in desperate circumstances. We might feel totally unprepared and ill-equipped to deal with these situations. We might feel afraid, helpless or even hopeless. But the Bible reminds us that we are God's handiwork. We are those on whom God has set His seal and in whom He has placed His Spirit. We are called to imitate Christ to our neighbour. And the key to doing the greatest of good works is to look beyond the situation to the person and to love as Jesus loved. Good works have been prepared in advance for us to do. We enter into them not unprepared, but as those created and equipped to fulfil the task.

PRAYER

Thank You, O God, that You have given me Your Holy Spirit so that I might be able to love as Jesus loved. Please help me, with eyes open and heart tender, to offer myself to You that I might do Your will and bring You glory. I pray that You would help me to not be afraid of touching the pain of others, that I might see their healing in Jesus' name. Thank You too for the church in Kurdistan and for the mighty things You are accomplishing through Your servants there, who love as Jesus loved.

DAY 88

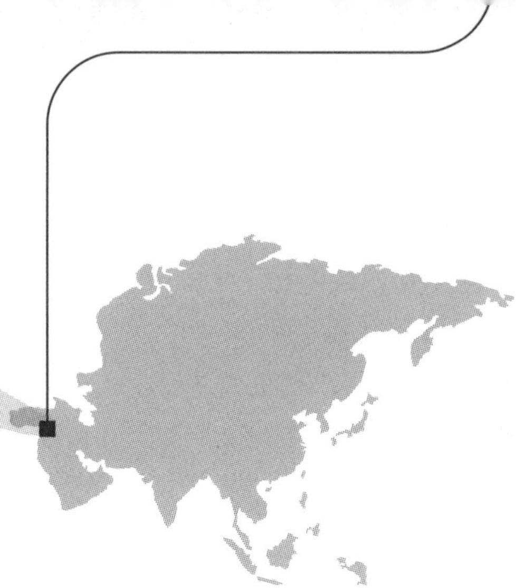

SYRIA

Part 1

As you reach your final destination, it is patently clear that your journey will not end in comfort or enjoyment. In fact, the situation here is so desperate that you have not been able to find a legal avenue into the country, with land borders closed and commercial flights scarce. Instead, you are stuck at the border.

You feel sad that a place with so much biblical heritage has come to this. Until recently, free healthcare and education were provided and the nation was growing thanks to agriculture, tourism and the oil industry. Today, its buildings are destroyed and its people have been scattered. Over five million fled the country after civil war broke out in 2011, with the vast majority now residing in Turkey or other nations of the Middle East. Most live in informal communities rather than refugee camps, with limited access to basic necessities. Families huddle around campfires of burning litter, and young children long desperately to play with a ball or toy. Meanwhile, their older siblings search for items to trade to help the family get by. Another six million Syrians are thought to be displaced within their own country.

Hundreds of thousands lost their lives in the conflict here as radical Islamic groups tore the nation apart. Hamza, a refugee, describes plumes of smoke, ruined buildings and gunfire. By the time he left Damascus, once busy roads were emptied, shop fronts were shuttered and only a handful of shoes were laid outside the doors of the mosques. Syria had become a nation in hiding.

BIBLE VERSE

'"You have lifted up the shrine of your king, the pedestal of your idols, the star of your god – which you made for yourselves. Therefore I will send you into exile beyond Damascus," says the Lord, whose name is God Almighty'
(Amos 5:26–27).

REFLECTION

Some are tempted to attribute all unrest and suffering to God's judgment, assuming that His wrath is being poured out. Jesus corrects such thinking in Luke 13, declaring that those killed by the falling tower of Siloam were no more guilty than others. And yet we cannot swing the other way and declare that God is absent, as Scripture plainly teaches His sovereignty and often speaks of His judgment. He judged Egypt and her gods (Ex. 12:12), Edom (Ezek. 35), Assyria (Is. 10:5–19) and Babylon (Is. 13), to name a few. In Amos 5, we even see God's judgment against Israel. We cannot say why modern-day Syria faces such struggles. Evil hearts are involved, yet the Lord is sovereign. But may our hearts break for the vulnerable, cry out for justice and long for peace, and may we follow the Lord's call in Amos 5:4: 'Seek me and live'.

PRAYER

Sovereign Lord, I pray for the nation of Syria and all those who have lost homes, jobs and possessions. I grieve with those who have lost loved ones. Please protect those who have been widowed, orphaned, injured and impoverished. Please provide for those who are living in unsafe situations with little access to basic necessities. I pray that You would bring peace to the nation and hope to its people, not only through the country's restoration but ultimately through the good news of Christ the Saviour. I pray that many Syrians would seek You and live.

DAY 89

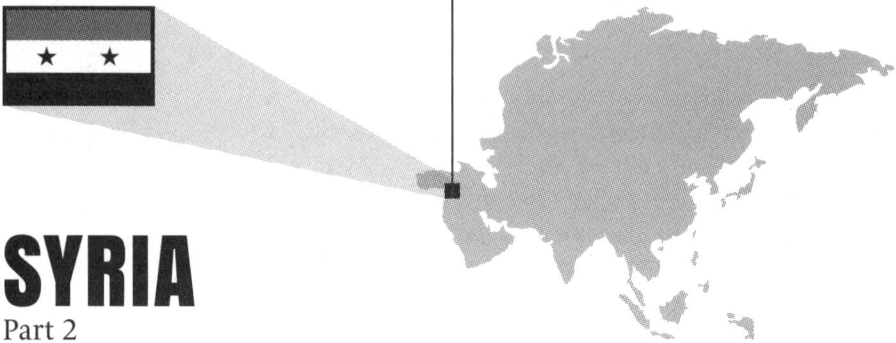

SYRIA
Part 2

You still cannot comprehend ten million people being displaced from their homes and wonder if there is any hope for these exiles. Then you meet Adil. He is 20 now but was a teenager when his parents died in the war. He is living with his older siblings in a 'village' where rows of makeshift tents barely exclude the rain, let alone the cold. He explains that he had spent several years wondering why he faced such hardship. His family were good people and he had always sought to please God. He said his prayers, fasted, was generous and did not drink. Why was his city in ruins too? Was this truly God's will?

However, something changed a few months ago. Having had rare access to a charging point, Adil was searching for information on his phone when he noticed an advert for the 'holy books', mentioned in the Quran. Over the following weeks, as his battery allowed, he read through them and eventually reached the Injil (New Testament). It was there that he finally saw where God's plans were heading. He had heard of Isa al-Masih (Jesus the Messiah) before, but only now did Jesus' suffering make sense. Adil saw that Jesus came to end oppression and suffering through the judgment of the wicked, the forgiveness of the repentant and the restoration of all things. He welcomed Jesus into his life soon after, but has not yet told his siblings.

Adil is praying that God would lead him to another believer in the village soon. He asks you to pray for him, and for his siblings and all Syrians who follow the teachings of Islam. He longs for them to meet Jesus.

BIBLE VERSE

'Blessed are the poor in spirit, for theirs is the kingdom of heaven' (Mt. 5:3).

REFLECTION

How often do we long to see successful, popular, famous or influential Christians, assuming that this will be good for God's kingdom and glory? Jesus teaches something quite contrary – that the poor in spirit are the ones to whom the kingdom of heaven belongs. We hear talk of 'strategic' ministries directed towards influential cities and individuals, but we must never lose sight of the poor in spirit, the meek or those who mourn. James 1:26–27 reminds us that pure and faultless religion is not having theological qualifications or being involved with impressive international movements. It is controlling our tongues, looking after orphans and widows, and keeping ourselves from being polluted by the world. Do you share God's heart for orphans like Adil, and for the many families like his around the world today who are poor in spirit? Do you long for them to meet Jesus?

PRAYER

Lord, thank You that all who come to You through faith in Jesus can know You as their Father. I praise You for the miracle You worked in Adil's life and for the many others who have discovered Your Word through digital media, with no Christian around and no Bible to hand. Please continue to work powerfully through digital ministries, bringing truth to those who have never heard the gospel, particularly in places where Bibles are unavailable. And Lord, please help me to know what it is to be poor in spirit, that I might delight all the more in Your kingdom.

DAY OF REFLECTION

It has been three months since you set off and the journey before you began to sink in. You envisaged the places you would go, the people you would meet and the challenges you would encounter. Ninety days later, the journey is complete. It has included 27 countries, dozens of churches, and thousands of brothers and sisters in Christ. You have met inspiring workers who passionately share the gospel among people who have never heard of Christ. Sometimes this has been big, open proclamation to eager listeners, but it has usually taken place in smaller, day-to-day conversations, often against the background of opposition and oppression.

You have met churches who rejoice in God's Word and pastors who long for access to it. You have visited places where people have everything this world can offer, and places where people have nothing at all. Perhaps you have learned innumerable lessons from the Lord, or perhaps God has been reminding you of things you already knew. Perhaps everything you have done, seen and heard has reinforced the simple truth upon which you first reflected – that the Word of the Lord is right and true; that He is faithful in all He does; that He loves righteousness and justice; and that the earth is full of His unfailing love (Ps. 33:4–5).

Just because you are on your way home does not mean that the journey is over. Which places and people stood out to you? Which parts were the most encouraging, the most surprising and the most challenging? Which of the things you have discovered in this book will you take into the days and months ahead? How does God want you to respond?

BIBLE VERSE

'... the earth is full of his unfailing love' (Ps. 33:5).

REFLECTION

As we saw back at the start of the journey, Psalm 33 depicts God's sovereign rule over all things. The heavens and the earth were formed by His Word; He is in control from the stars in the sky to the waters of the sea (vv. 6–9). But the psalm does not lay out these truths simply to teach us. Rather, we are called to sing (vv. 1, 3), to praise (v. 2), and to fear and revere the Lord (v. 8). This call applies not only to God's people, but to all the earth – to every person who lives in the world He created. The earth is full of God's unfailing love; He is truly worthy of our reverence and our praise. From Syria to Sri Lanka and from Mongolia to Malaysia, may the people of Asia praise Him!

PRAYER

Thank You, Lord, for this journey! Thank You for raising up gospel workers across the continent of Asia and for every individual who acknowledges Jesus as Lord, whether they worship freely or in secret. Please sustain those who lack fellowship, and provide for those in need. Lord, enable Your church to bless every Asian nation as they worship You in word and deed, living out the joy of being Your children. Please provide Bibles where there are none and send gospel workers to those who remain unreached. Lord, please help me to see what role I can play. Above all, please bring glory to Your name as the power of Jesus transforms lives in Asia.